The History and Function of Property Exemptions in Oklahoma Law

by James M. Branum

I0390928

ᏔᎹᎾᏆᎵ ᏗᎮᎢᏍᏣᎦᏴᎩ
Green Corn Press

The History and Function of Oklahoma Property Exemptions

Green Corn Press, PO Box 721016, Oklahoma City, OK 73172
www.GreenCornPress.com

Printings:
- 2012 CLE Presentation Handout for the Bankruptcy Section of the Oklahoma County Bar Association
- Lulu.com Print on Demand - ISBN: 978-1-300-31841-5

Electronic Releases:
- Lulu.com Epub and other formats- ISBN:
- Kindle - ASIN:
- Smashwords – ISBN: 9781301325528

Disclaimer: This book is not a substitute for individualized legal advice from an attorney. I have done my best to give you useful, accurate legal information, but that's not the same as personalized legal advice. If you are not an attorney and want help understanding how the law applies to your particular circumstances, you should consider seeing a qualified attorney.

Special Thanks

I want to thank Professor Richard Coulson for his invaluable assistance on the original version of this work. I also want to thank my father, James R. Branum for his comments on later rewrites of this work.

Table of Contents

Chapter 3. Conclusions and Suggestions for Change

Appendices:

About the Author

Other Books Available from Green Corn Press

Preface

I wrote this paper originally as a directed research project during my last semester of law school, a short-time after the enactment of the Bankruptcy Abuse Prevention and Consumer Protection Act of 2005 (BAPCPA).[1] At that time, I believed that the fallout out of the passage of BAPCPA would be the central issue for policymakers when it came to bankruptcy exemption laws. What I did not foresee then, was that the world was about to enter a financial crisis that bore many similarities to the economic turmoil of early Oklahoma history.[2] It is because of these current issues

---

[1] Marc Stern, A *Primer on Sweeping Bankruptcy Reform*, GP|SOLO LAW TRENDS & NEWS PRACTICE AREA NEWSLETTER, & 1 (August 2005) *available at:* http://www.abanet.org/genpractice/newsletter/lawtrends/ 0508/business/bankruptcy.html
.

[2] Most of us are well-familiar with Oklahoma's dark days of the Dust Bowl and The Great Depression. What most of us do not realize is that the majority of working-class Oklahomans were experiencing wretched poverty long before the Great Crash of '29. One good source for discussion of the economic

that I decided to rewrite this paper and turn it into a small book. My hope is that by understanding our history (both what has worked and what has not worked), we will better understand what changes could and should be made in our current exemption laws.

While this book will focus on the story of Oklahoma's exemption scheme, the comparative analysis of other states' bankruptcy exemptions may be useful to readers in other states as well.

---

conditions of the early statehood era can be found in JIM BISSETT, AGRARIAN SOCIALISM IN AMERICA: MARX, JEFFERSON AND JESUS IN THE OKLAHOMA COUNTRYSIDE 1903-1920 (UNIVERSITY OF OKLAHOMA PRESS 1999).

Introduction

The US Constitution gave Congress the unfettered authority to set uniform bankruptcy laws in the United States[3]. Under such power, Congress could have established a single set of property exemptions for the entire nation. Instead, however, bankruptcy law in the United States has for almost all of its post-civil war modern history (from 1867-1878, and from 1898-to date)[4] allowed the respective state legislatures to play a role in setting the balance between creditor and debtor interests, through the drafting of their own exemption schemes.

Given the Congressional intention of allowing states to play this balance-setting role, this paper will explore exactly what

---

[3] U.S. CONST. art. I, § 8, cl. 3.

[4] Mark Glick, LAW AND ECONOMICS SOCIETY OF THE UNIVERSITY OF UTAH, A HISTORY OF CORPORATE BANKRUPTCY, *available at:* whttp://ww.econ.utah.edu/les/version_2.0/papers/A History of Corporate Bankruptcy.htm

balance the Oklahoma exemptions were designed to set, whether that balance was actually met through the exemptions in the past, and whether the exemptions actually function to serve this legislatively intended balance today. The primary focus of the paper will be historical in nature, but will also provide some comparison between the functionality of the Oklahoma exemptions in comparison with the exemptions of two other states, both in and out of the bankruptcy context.

One other point worth noting is that the contours of bankruptcy law have radically changed since the passage of BAPCPA in 2005[5]. In several ways BAPCPA has upset the traditional federal-state balance of powers in the bankruptcy context: (1) by placing a cap on homestead exemptions in many circumstances (debtors who have established a new domicile within the last 730 days must follow the rules of 11 USCA

---

[5]Marc Stern, A *Primer on Sweeping Bankruptcy Reform*, GP|SOLO LAW TRENDS & NEWS PRACTICE AREA NEWSLETTER, & 1 (August 2005) *available at:* http://www.abanet.org/genpractice/newsletter/lawtrends/ 0508/business/bankruptcy.html.

522(b)[6], while debtors who have been a domicile of their current state of residence for more than 730 days but who acquired their non-family farm[7] homestead less than 1,215 days prior to filing, have a maximum homestead cap of \$136,875 on the applicable homestead that otherwise would be in place under that state's law[8]), (2) by reducing the access of the debtor to chapter 7 bankruptcy in which the state exemptions function to protect debtor's property from being taken to satisfy the debtor's obligations,[9] and (3)by requiring debtors in bankruptcy to use the exemptions of the state where they were domiciled 730 days ago and not those of the state they currently reside in.[10] This last issue raises special problems since many states (including Oklahoma[11]) do not permit current non-residents to enjoy the benefits of their particular exemption laws.[12]

---

[6] 11 U.S.C.A. § 522(b) (2005).

[7] 11 U.S.C.A. § 522(p)(2) (2005).

[8] 11 U.S.C.A. § 522(p)(1) (2005).

[9] 11 U.S.C.A. § 522(b)(4) (2005).

[10] 11 U.S.C.A. § 522 (b)(3)(A) (2005).

[11] OKLA. STAT. ANN. Tit. 31 § 1 (A) (2012).

[12] For a summary of the various state laws on this

Given these changes that have served to limit the power of state legislatures to set the balance they might otherwise have desired to set, one might wonder if state bankruptcy exemption law is even a worthy area of inquiry. I would argue that despite these changes, state exemption law still serves a significant role in several key ways: (1) Since many future bankruptcy debtors are now forced to file for chapter 13 protection, the exemptions will be needed to calculate the "best interests of the creditors" test, which requires that a chapter 13 plan must provide the unsecured creditors at least as much proceeds as they would have received in a chapter 7 bankruptcy[13], (2) a significant number of Oklahoma debtors would still be eligible to receive the benefits of the unlimited homestead exemption since they acquired their homestead more than 1,215 days ago, and (3) since many debtors will be barred from filing bankruptcy altogether (for exceeding the chapter 7 means test[14] while

---

issue, *see* http://www.exemptionsexpress.com.
[13] 11 U.S.C.A. § 1325(a)(4) (2005).

at the same time being unable to construct a workable chapter 13 plan[15]) the use of exemption law outside of bankruptcy to protect a debtor's important assets will likely increase (and outside of bankruptcy, provisions such as the Code's cap on the value of homesteads, and the restrictions on the use of state exemptions by people who have recently moved to a state, will not be a challenge[16]

Oklahoma's property exemption laws are found in two sources: the state constitution (which provides for the homestead exemption[17]) and statutes (which provide for both the homestead and personal property exemptions).[18] The provisions of

---

[14] 11 U.S.C.A. § 522(b)(2) (2005).

[15] 11 U.S.C.A. § 1325 (2005).

[16]One interesting issue is the question of why Congress has effectively placed people who frequently change domiciles under two sets of exemptions – one set of exemptions to protect their assets outside of bankruptcy, with a second set of exemptions to protect their assets if they file bankruptcy. It is very possible that these two sets of exemptions could create some rather interesting and likely unexpected results.

[17] OKLA. CONST. Art. 12

the constitution and statutes are given further meaning by the decisions of Oklahoma state courts and federal bankruptcy courts; the exemptions are also limited in scope in the context of bankruptcy by the recent revisions to the federal bankruptcy code. It is also important to remember that the exemptions also function outside of bankruptcy (without the recent limitations of the bankruptcy code revisions), to prevent creditors from execution against exempt property.

---

[18] OKLA. STAT. ANN. Tit. 31

Chapter 1: The Historical Evolution of Oklahoma's Exemption laws

A. Exemption provisions in the State constitution

The forces that influenced the Oklahoma state constitutional convention in its decision dto draft the state's generous homestead exemption provisions can be traced over the decades prior to its adoption, beginning first with the innovation of the Homestead Exemption in Texas, the Indian Removals and later opening of Indian Territory to non-Indian settlement, the creation of exemption laws for the Twin Territories by way of the Organic Act, the debate over statehood, the experience of the Sequoyah convention in 1905, and finally the Oklahoma State constitutional convention itself. This next section will explore in more depth these factors and how they shaped the eventual Oklahoma exemption laws.

1. 1819-1889 – Oklahoma

The early history of US involvement in Oklahoma is a complicated story[19], with the territory being first brought into the United States as part of the Louisiana Territory, then later the Missouri Territory, then later the Arkansas Territory beginning in 1819.[20] [21] Most of present-day Oklahoma was separated from Arkansas territory in 1824.

Two county governments were established by the Arkansas Territory in the territory's remaining parts of what would later become Oklahoma: Lovely County (founded in 1827 but lasting for only one

---

[19]This book will unfortunately not discuss any possible property exemption laws found under tribal or colonial governments in present-day Oklahoma before the Louisiana Purchase of 1803.

[20]https://en.wikipedia.org/wiki/History_of_Oklahoma

[21]A map showing the boundaries of the Arkansas Territory in different eras can be found at Map 3 in Appendix C of this book.

year)[22] [23] [24] and Miller County (founded in 1820, but losing the Oklahoma portion of its lands in 1828)[25]. While there likely some kind of exemption statutes that would have been binding in these territorial counties, they likely had little if any real impact on future developments in Oklahoma exemption laws. With regards to constitutional history, Arkansas Territory's government was established and governed by an act of congress in 1819, but this act did not set up any kind of property exemption scheme.[26]

---

[22]*See Lovely County, Arkansas Territory* WIKIPEDIA (2012) *AVAILABLE AT:*
https://en.wikipedia.org/wiki/Lovely_County,_Arkansas_Territory .

[23]*See Lovely County, Arkansas* ROOTSWEB (2012) *AVAILABLE AT:*http://www.rootsweb.ancestry.com/~arwcags/LovelyCountyArkansas/LovelyCounty1.htm .

[24]*See Lovely County* ENCYCLOPEDIA OF ARKANSAS (2012) *AVAILABLE AT:*http://www.encyclopediaofarkansas.net/encyclopedia/entry-detail.aspx?entryID=2940 .

[25] *See Miller County, Arkansas Territory* WIKIPEDIA (2012) *AVAILABLE AT:*
https://en.wikipedia.org/wiki/Miller_County,_Arkansas_Territory

[26] "An act establishing a separate territorial

The next step in the evolution of Oklahoma laws began in 1839, when the Republic of Texas created a homestead exemption for 50 acres of land or one town lot with improvements (worth up to $500, the equivalent of $12,500 in 2010 dollars[27] [28]), a measure designed by Texas to attract settlers from the United States (an attractive proposition since many settlers to Texas were folks were fleeing from creditors back East, as noted by a Wisconsin commentator of the era who said that the homestead law made Texas "a noted asylum for all of the desperadoes of the country"[29]).

---

government in the southern part of the territory of Missouri of 1819" reprinted in *The Federal and state constitutions, colonial charters, and other organic laws of the state, territories, and colonies now or heretofore forming the United States of America* (1909) p. 261- 264 *AVAILABLE AT:* http://archive.org/stream/cu31924019912025#page/n301/mode/2up

[27] *See* Appendix B.

[28] *See* Paul Goodman, *The Emergence of Homestead Exemption: Accommodation and resistance to the Market revolution, 1840-1880*, JOURNAL OF AMERICAN HISTORY 470 (Sep. 1993).

[29] *See id.* 478.

Also, another provision of the Texas statute that was designed to attract new settlement was a provision in the Texas homestead law that prohibited a husband from selling the family homestead without his wife's consent, which likely made Texas a more attractive place to move to, for the wives of settlers who might be otherwise reluctant to move to the frontier.[30]

---

[30] *See id.* 477.

Interestingly, the Texas homestead exemption laws actually would have been the law of the land in two parts of Oklahoma in the years following 1839: the present-day Oklahoma panhandle was part of Texas until 1850[31], and a considerable portion of present-day far Southwestern Oklahoma (Greer County) was arguably part of Texas until 1896[32] (see map 1 in the

---

[31] *See Oklahoma Panhandle* WIKIPEDIA (2005) *AVAILABLE AT:* http://en.wikipedia.org/wiki/ Oklahoma_Pandhandle, *also see generally* Emma Estill-Harbour, *Greer County*, CHRONICLES OF OKLAHOMA (June 1934) *AVAILABLE AT:* http://digital.library.okstate.edu/Chronicles/v012/v01 2p145.html, Webb L. Moore *Greer County*, TEXAS HANDBOOK ONLINE (2005) *AVAILABLE AT:* http://www.tsha.utexas.edu/handbook/online/articles/ GG/hcg81.html. The present-day Oklahoma panhandle was part of the Republic and later of state of Texas until Texas sold a disputed part of its northernmost territory (including the present-day Oklahoma panhandle) for the sum of $10 million.
[32] Greer County v. State of Texas, 197 U.S. 235, 243 (1997) *AVAILABLE AT* http://www.law.cornell.edu/supremecourt/text/197/23 5 . I say arguably because while the Republic and later State of Texas claimed this area, the US Supreme Court held in the Greer County case that it never was part of Texas. Justice Holmes said in this opinion that : "It was a discovery that the state of Texas never had had a title to the land known as

appendices). These laws however would not have had any practical effect in the present-day Panhandle[33], but the portion of former Texas-territory in Oklahoma would have seen the exemptions function for a short time.

At the time of its formation by the Texas legislature in 1860, Greer County's expansive territory[34] consisted of what

---

Greer county. The United States found itself at liberty to do what it chose with that land. It could have done nothing. It could have subdivided it at will. It could have made it part of some existing county. The land and its inhabitants retained no legal personality, least of all that personality with which Texas had purported to endow them."

[33] *See* Clarke, Fannie McAlpine, *A Chapter in the History of Young Territory*, SOUTHWESTERN HISTORICAL QUARTERLY ONLINE 31 (1906, 2005) *AVAILABLE AT:* http://www.tsha.utexas.edu/publications/journals/shq/online/v009/n1/article_6.html, *also see Oklahoma Panhandle* WIKIPEDIA (2005) *AVAILABLE AT:* http://en.wikipedia.org/wiki/ Oklahoma_Pandhandle. The present-day Oklahoma panhandle was not settled by non-American Indians in 1850, which means that the Texas homestead exemption law would have had no practical effect in this area.

[34] Clarke, Fannie McAlpine, *A Chapter in the History of Young Territory*, SOUTHWESTERN HISTORICAL

would later become three Oklahoma Counties (Greer, Jackson County, and Harmon), as well as portions of Beckham County in Oklahoma and Lipscomb, Hemphill, Wheeler, Collingsworth and Childress counties in Texas (these Texas counties would be later created by the Texas legislature in 1876, from a portion of land removed from Greer County's jurisdiction as well as the nearby Young's Territory.[35]

Due to the outbreak of the American Civil War, Greer County remained unsettled[36] and unorganized until the 1870's when ranchers first began to run cattle in the county. By 1881 the vacuum of "law and order" in Greer County was filled when the county as attached to Wheeler County for judicial purposes.[37] A few years later in 1886

QUARTERLY ONLINE 31 (1906, 2005) *AVAILABLE AT:* http://www.tsha.utexas.edu/publications/journals/shq/online/v009/n1/article_6.html. Prior to 1860 this area was part of the unorganized "Young's Territory" which had been set aside as an Indian reservation.
[35] *See id.*

[36]David Morgan, *Greer County, Texas Feb 8, 1860 - Mar 16, 1896,* TX GENWEB (1998, 2005) *AVAILABLE AT:* http://www.rootsweb.com/~txgreer/.

residents of Greer County legally established their own government and courts by way of a petition and election process provided by state law.[38]

By the time that Greer County had formed its own county government, a serious cloud of doubt had risen over whether Texas's claim to jurisdiction was valid or not (and more importantly to Greer County residents, a cloud over the land titles issued by Texas) based on the issue of which river was in fact the northern boundary of Texas.

---

[37] Susan Cabanniss Bradford, *History of Greer County* OK GENWEB PROJECT (1999, 2005) *AVAILABLE AT:*
http://freepages.genealogy.rootsweb.com/~swokla/greer/greer.html

[38] *see generally* Susan Cabanniss Bradford, *History of Greer County* OK GENWEB PROJECT (1999, 2005) *AVAILABLE AT:*
http://freepages.genealogy.rootsweb.com/~swokla/greer/greer.html; David Morgan, *Greer County, Texas Feb 8, 1860 - Mar 16, 1896,* TX GENWEB (1998, 2005) *AVAILABLE AT:*
http://www.rootsweb.com/~txgreer/; Emma Estill-Harbour, *Greer County*, Chronicles of Oklahoma (June 1934) *AVAILABLE AT:*
http://digital.library.okstate.edu/Chronicles/v012/v012p145.html.

In response to this uncertainty the county did not collect property taxes during this era (even though those holding title to land in Greer County under Texas law sought to pay those taxes to solidify their claim to the lands for which they held title) and remained in something of a state of limbo[39], until 1896 when Texas lost the case of United States vs. State of Texas[40] at the U.S. Supreme Court. Following this ruling, Congress created Greer County in Oklahoma Territory (with the former county officeholders being placed in office temporarily in the newly created Oklahoma territorial county until new elections were held)[41].

---

[39] Susan Cabanniss Bradford, *History of Greer County* OK GENWEB PROJECT (1999, 2005)
AVAILABLE AT:
http://freepages.genealogy.rootsweb.com/~swokla/greer/greer.html
[40] United States vs. State of Texas, 162 U.S. 1 (1896).
[41] Susan Cabanniss Bradford, *History of Greer County* OK GENWEB PROJECT (1999, 2005)
AVAILABLE AT:
http://freepages.genealogy.rootsweb.com/~swokla/greer/greer.html

While the Texas Homestead Exemption law had effectively been law in Greer County for a decade, the law's primary effect with regards to current Oklahoma law was one of indirect influence, as the concept of the Homestead exemption was adopted by many states across the US. This movement spread from Texas into the lower south, from there into the earlier settled portions of the country and finally into the Far West territories.[42] Proof of this growing trend could be found in looking at the number of states that had adopted the exemptions during this era: 45% of the United States had adopted the Homestead Exemption innovation by 1850[43] and by 1883 more than

---

[42] Paul Goodman, *The Emergence of Homestead Exemption: Accommodation and resistance to the Market revolution, 1840-1880*, JOURNAL OF AMERICAN HISTORY 470 (Sep. 1993).

[43] *Id.* at 472 (Sep. 1993), *also see List of U.S. states by date of Statehood* WIKIPEDIA (2005) *AVAILABLE AT:* http://en.wikipedia.org/wiki/List_of_U.S._states_by_date_of_statehood. 14 out of 31 United States had adopted the Homestead Exemption: Texas, Connecticut, Maine, Vermont, Pennsylvania, New York, Georgia, Mississippi, Alabama, Florida, Michigan, Wisconsin, Ohio, and Iowa.

85% of the United States[44] (as well eight United States territories[45]) had adopted the homestead exemption.

Along with the widespread general adoption of the Homestead Exemption, came another trend, a move during the post-reconstruction era to add generous

---

[44] *see* Paul Goodman, *The Emergence of Homestead Exemption: Accommodation and resistance to the Market revolution, 1840-1880*, JOURNAL OF AMERICAN HISTORY 470, 472 (Sep. 1993), *also see List of U.S. states by date of Statehood* WIKIPEDIA (2005) *AVAILABLE AT:* http://en.wikipedia.org/wiki/List_of_U.S._states_by_date_of_statehood. 33 out of 38 United States had adopted the Homestead Exemption: Texas, Maine, Vermont, Pennsylvania, New York, Georgia, Mississippi, Alabama, Florida, Michigan, Wisconsin, Ohio, Iowa, Massachusetts, New Hampshire, New Jersey, South Carolina, Louisiana, Tennessee, Arkansas, North Carolina, Missouri, West Virginia, Kentucky, Virginia, Illinois, Indiana, Kansas, Nebraska, Minnesota, California, Colorado, and Nevada.

[45] Paul Goodman, *The Emergence of Homestead Exemption: Accommodation and resistance to the Market revolution, 1840-1880*, JOURNAL OF AMERICAN HISTORY 470, 472 (Sep. 1993). Eight U.S. Territories had adopted the Homestead Exemption by 1883: Washington, Dakota, Idaho, Arizona, Montana, Wyoming, Utah, and New Mexico.

farm-friendly (with large acreage limits) to state constitutions (the approach used by Oklahoma today), with many jurisdictions exempting 80 or more acres of land by 1883.[46] Several of these states later played roles of influence in the eventual drafting of Oklahoma's exemptions: Kansas (the Kansas Constitution's homestead exemption provision was cited by a delegate to the Oklahoma Constitutional Convention in the proposition he was proposing for Oklahoma's constitutional exemption[47]), Texas (both because of its vicinity and because as discussed earlier, portions of what would be come Oklahoma were at this time still claimed by Texas[48]) and Arkansas

---

[46] *Id.* at 472 United States and Territories exempting more than 80 acres of land without a valuation cap in 1883 were: Texas, Mississippi, Alabama, Florida, Arkansas, Missouri, Kansas, Dakota and Montana.

[47] Proposition 66, Okla. Const. Convention (Dec. 3, 1906), *MICROFILMED ON:* Okla. Const. Convention tapes, Okla. Historical Society Library. This proposition ends with the language "Reference – Constitution of Kansas."

[48] *See Oklahoma Panhandle* WIKIPEDIA (2005) *AVAILABLE AT:* http://en.wikipedia.org/wiki/ Oklahoma_Pandhandle, *also see generally* Emma Estill-Harbour, *Greer County*, CHRONICLES OF

(Arkansas's exemption laws protected residents of Indian Territory from 1889-1907,[49] that as I will discuss later, likely was a brooding legislative influence over both the Sequoyah and later Oklahoma conventions' adoption of generous Homestead Exemptions).

In the same era that the Republic of Texas first adopted the Homestead Exemption, the tragic removals of American Indian peoples from the Southeastern United States to the Indian Territory was underway, in which the citizens of the Cherokee (Tsalagi), Chickasaw, Creek (Muskogee), Choctaw, and Seminole nations (the so-called "Five Civilized Tribes"[50]) were removed at

---

OKLAHOMA (June 1934) *AVAILABLE AT:* http://digital.library.okstate.edu/Chronicles/v012/v012p145.html, Webb L. Moore *Greer County*, TEXAS HANDBOOK ONLINE (2005) *AVAILABLE AT:* http://www.tsha.utexas.edu/handbook/online/articles/GG/hcg81.html. The present-day Oklahoma panhandle was part of the Republic and later of state of Texas until Texas sold a disputed part of its northernmost territory (including the present-day Oklahoma panhandle) for the sum of $10 million.
[49] 26 Stat. 81 § 31 (1890).
[50] *see generally* 26 Stat. 81 (1890). The term "Five

gunpoint by the U.S. Army from their homelands to the Indian Territory during the 1830's.[51] These forced removals began with the Choctaw Nation in 1831[52] and ended with the last of the Cherokee removals in 1838.[53] (Many other Indian tribes were later removed to present-day Oklahoma, but these removals occurred after the American Civil War when land was taken from the Five Civilized Tribes as part of the Reconstruction Treaties.[54])

Upon settlement in Oklahoma, the tribes faced serious hardships but gradually

---

civilized tribes" is used in this book as a term of art. This term is arguably offensive since it implies that the other tribes were not "civilized." My usage of this term in this book should not be seen as an endorsement of this implication but rather should be read as a legal term of art in a particular historical context, particularly as it was used by the Oklahoma Organic Act cited here.

[51]Portions of some of these tribes also voluntarily migrated westward, some to what would be come Oklahoma, others to portions of Arkansas.

[52] VICTOR E. HARLOW, HARLOW'S OKLAHOMA HISTORY 73-74 (Arrell M. Gibson ed. Harlow Publishing Corp. 1967) (1934).

[53] *Id.* at 92.

[54] *Id.* at 153.

rebuilt their communities, social and governmental structures and ways of life. During this time period the tribes continued their traditional practice of communal land ownership (in which the tribe retained title to all tribal lands but individual members owned the improvements upon the land[55])

---

[55]An example of this is found in the Cherokee Nation Constitution of 1839, Article I, Section 2 AVAILABLE AT http://www.cherokeeobserver.org/Issues/1839constitution.html, which provides that "The lands of the Cherokee Nation shall remain common property; but the improvements made thereon, and in the possession of the citizens respectively who made, or may rightfully be in possession of them: Provided, that the citizens of the Nation possessing exclusive and indefeasible right to their improvements, as expressed in this article, shall possess no right or power to dispose of their improvements, in any manner whatever, to the United States, individual States, or to individual citizens thereof; and that, whenever any citizen shall remove with his effects out of the limits of this Nation, and become a citizen of any other government, all his rights and privileges as a citizen of this Nation shall cease: Provided, nevertheless, That the National Council shall have power to re-admit, by law, to all the rights of citizenship, any such person or persons who may, at any time, desire to return to the Nation, on memorializing the National Council for such readmission."

which created a very different socio-economic structure than that which existed in the outside world.[56] (which includes the lack of a need for homestead exemption laws in Indian Territory since there would be no privately held homesteads to protect in what is now Oklahoma, with the exception of those portions of territory that were at this time still claimed as Texas territory.[57] [58])

---

[56] DANNEY GOBLE, PROGRESSIVE OKLAHOMA: THE MAKING OF A NEW KIND OF STATE 66-67 (University of Oklahoma Press 1980).

[57] *See Oklahoma Panhandle* WIKIPEDIA (2005) *AVAILABLE AT:* http://en.wikipedia.org/wiki/ Oklahoma_Pandhandle, *also see generally* Emma Estill-Harbour, *Greer County*, CHRONICLES OF OKLAHOMA (June 1934) *AVAILABLE AT:* http://digital.library.okstate.edu/Chronicles/v012/v01 2p145.html, Webb L. Moore *Greer County*, TEXAS HANDBOOK ONLINE (2005) *AVAILABLE AT:* http://www.tsha.utexas.edu/handbook/online/articles/ GG/hcg81.html. The present-day Oklahoma panhandle was part of the Republic and later of state of Texas until Texas sold a disputed part of its northernmost territory (including the present-day Oklahoma panhandle) for the sum of $10 million. [58] One area of inquiry that is beyond the scope of this book is whether the Five Civilized Tribes drafted exemption laws to cover personal property and

The American Civil War seriously disrupted the tribes' existence in Indian Territory. Most tribal governments ended up aligning themselves with the Confederacy (in part due to those tribes' practice of legal slavery, as well as their fears over Lincoln's stated policy of pushing for expanded white settlement in the west) but individual tribal members were split in their allegiances between the North and the South, with some tribes having significant pro-Union factions.[59]

Following the cessation of hostilities, the U.S. Federal government coerced the tribal governments of Indian Territory into signing new treaties in which the tribes agreed to give up much of their land holdings (primarily in Western Oklahoma) as punishment for their siding with the Southern rebellion.[60] This turn of events set

---

privately-owned improvements upon the communally held lands. I hope to discuss this issue in future revisions/updates of this book.

[59] *See generally* VICTOR E. HARLOW, HARLOW'S OKLAHOMA HISTORY 127-152 (Arrell M. Gibson ed. Harlow Publishing Corp. 1967) (1934).

the stage for the removals of additional Indian tribes to these newly acquired federal territories[61], and to the immigration of large numbers of non-Indian settlers into Western and Central Oklahoma, beginning with the opening of the Unassigned Lands in 1889.[62]

By this time significant numbers of non-Indians were present in Indian Territory and their number rapidly increased. Black Americans had already been present in the territory (many remaining after emancipation from slavery, in some cases even being adopted as citizens by the tribes[63]), and some White Americans had secured tribal citizenship by means of intermarriage or by being of mixed Indian and White ancestry.[64] Many White Americans were also present in Indian Territory unlawfully during this era as well.[65]

---

[60] *See generally id.* 153-163.

[61] *See generally id.* 164-179.

[62] *See generally id.* 204-208.

[63] *See generally id.* 183-184.

[64] DANNEY GOBLE, PROGRESSIVE OKLAHOMA: THE MAKING OF A NEW KIND OF STATE 48 (University of Oklahoma Press 1980).

2. 1890-1905 – The era of the Twin Territories

The post-Reconstruction socio-economic changes in Indian Territory and the perceived need for "law and order" brought the next significant change in law (which included exemption laws) in what is now Oklahoma. This came by way of the passage of the Organic Act of 1890[66]. The Act created Oklahoma Territory from "the portion of the United States now known as Indian Territory (except so much of the same as is actually occupied by the five civilized tribes, and the Indian tribes within the Quapaw Indian Agency, and except the unoccupied part of the Cherokee outlet),"[67] while Indian Territory would remain as a separate territory in Eastern Oklahoma but

---

[65] *Id.* at 184, *also see id.* at 66, *and see* VICTOR E. HARLOW, HARLOW'S OKLAHOMA HISTORY 238-240 (Arrell M. Gibson ed. Harlow Publishing Corp. 1967) (1934). By 1890, Indians only comprised 28% of the population in Oklahoma and by statehood this number had dropped to 9%.

[66] 26 Stat. 81 (1890).

[67] *See id.* § 1.

additional land could be removed from Indian Territory and placed under the jurisdiction of Oklahoma Territory if the Indian Nation or tribe in question assented to its addition to Oklahoma Territory if the applicable treaties required their accession.[68]

The new Oklahoma Territorial government consisted of an appointed governor[69] and secretary[70], an elected territorial legislative assembly[71], and a territorial court system[72] (but with law enforcement power remaining with the US Marshal[73]); Indian Territory would remain under a governmental mix of tribal jurisdiction, and US federal jurisdiction through the US district and circuit courts for Indian Territory, the Western District of Arkansas, and the Eastern district of Texas.[74]

---

[68] *See id.* § 1& 2.

[69] *See id.* § 2.

[70] *See id.* § 3.

[71] *See id.* § 2.

[72] *See id.* § 9.

[73] *See id.* § 1.

[74] *See generally* 26 Stat. 81 § 29-36 (1890).

With regards to exemption laws, the Organic Act[75] established that selected provisions of the general laws of the state of Arkansas would be in effect in Indian Territory, including chapter 60 (execution). Along with this, the Organic Act provided for a limited number of specific exemption provisions: (1) no attachments were allowed on improvements on real estate that had title vesting in an Indian nation (with a few exceptions for mining, railroads and other industry that was licensed by either the tribal government or the United States), and (2) executions obtained in non-Indian courts against the improvements owned by either an adopted citizen of a tribe or a non-citizen of a tribe, if said improvements were on land in excess of 160 acres.[76] This was significant as it provided a measure of exemption protection to persons who did not hold title to land (since prior to the Dawes allotments, land was held communally by the tribe and not by individuals[77]) but who had invested in improvements upon the land.[78]

---

[75] 26 Stat. 81 § 31 (1890).

[76] *See id.* § 31.

The Arkansas exemption statutes that were placed as law for Indian Territory were in fact fairly new in Arkansas, since the state's post-Reconstruction-era constitution (which still is Arkansas's constitution today) had only been ratified in 1874.[79] This constitution provided for property exemption within the text of the constitution, but these exemptions were also echoed in statute (these statutes are what became law in Indian Territory by way of the Organic Act). These Arkansas exemptions provided for a two-tiered system in which those who were not heads of families had only an exemption of $200 in personal property as well as unlimited amount of clothing[80], while heads of

---

[77] JIM BISSETT, AGRARIAN SOCIALISM IN AMERICA: MARX, JEFFERSON AND JESUS IN THE OKLAHOMA COUNTRYSIDE 1903-1920 17-18 (University of Oklahoma Press 1999).

[78] DANNEY GOBLE, PROGRESSIVE OKLAHOMA: THE MAKING OF A NEW KIND OF STATE 66 (University of Oklahoma Press 1980). This protection was important since in 1890 only 28% of the Indian Territory's population was American Indian, and by statehood this percentage was diluted to only 9%.

[79] *See generally* ARK. CONST.

families were entitled to an exemption of $500 in personal property, the clothing of the family[81] and the homestead exemption. This homestead exemption was limited to 160 acres of land "outside any city, town or village" (with improvements) valued up to $2500 or 80 acres of land of unlimited value[82], or 1 acre of urban real estate (with improvements) valued up to $2500 or ¼ acre of urban real estate of unlimited value.[83]

For the western part of what is now Oklahoma, the Organic Act placed Oklahoma territory under selected provisions of the statutory code for the state of Nebraska, which were to remain in effect for about one year, from November 1, 1889 until the adjournment of the first territorial legislative assembly.[84] This new temporary

---

[80] ARK. CONST. art. 9 § 1, *and see* ARK. STAT. § 2992 (1884).

[81] ARK. CONST. art. 9 § 2, *and see* ARK. STAT. § 2993 (1884).

[82] ARK. CONST. art. 9 § 4, *and see* ARK. STAT. § 2995 (1884).

[83] ARK. CONST. art. 9 § 5, *and see* ARK. STAT. § 2996 (1884).

[84] 26 Stat. 81 § 11 (1890).

territorial statutory code included Nebraska's homestead exemptions[85] as well as Nebraska's personal property exemptions which were provided in the state's Code of Civil Procedure.[86] The Nebraska homestead exemption provided for heads of families[87] a protected rural homestead of 160 acres (worth less than $2000) or a protected urban homestead that covered no more than 2 lots (with strangely no limitation in value).[88]

The Nebraska personal property exemptions took a unique approach, providing for no exemption provisions for non-heads of families, a wildcard exemption of $500 for heads of household who are not able to utilize the homestead exemption[89], as well as to provide for all

---

[85] NEB. STAT. 36 (1881).

[86] NEB. CODE OF CIVIL PROCEDURE § 520-531 (1881).

[87] NEB. STAT. 36 § 15 (1881). The Nebraska statute gave an expansive definition of the term "head of a family", extending it to cover both husbands as well as any other person who is caring for a child or dependent family member.

[88] NEB. STAT. 36 § 1 (1881).

[89] NEB. CODE OF CIVIL PROCEDURE § 521 (1881).

heads of families a laundry list of protected "articles of personality" (which include personal items, cemetery plots, clothing, furniture, live stock, a wagon, farm implements, six months of provisions and tools of the trade).[90]

The Nebraska exemptions did not remain law for every long, however, because the Oklahoma Territory Legislative Assembly drafted its own property exemptions which took effect on Dec. 25, 1890.[91]

The Oklahoma Territory (O.T.) property exemptions had much in common with the Nebraska exemptions in providing for generous homestead and property exemptions, however unlike Nebraska, the Oklahoma Territory exemptions did provide for a limited set of exemptions for non-heads of families.

The O.T. exemption provisions for heads of families included a homestead exemption similar to both Nebraska law and what

---

[90] *See id.* § 530.
[91] OKLA. TERRITORY STAT., 2860 § 1-5 (1890).

would eventually became law in the state of Oklahoma: 160 acre limit for rural homesteads and a 1 acre limit for urban homesteads[92], while the personal property exemptions for a family consisted of a hodge-podge list of items that is also fairly similar to both Nebraska law and future Oklahoma state exemption law.[93] [94]

For non-heads of household the exemptions under the Oklahoma Territory statute were limited to cemetery lots, clothing, tools of the trade, "one horse, bridge and saddle or one yoke of oxen", and current wages for personal property.[95]

3. 1905-1907 – The Sequoyah Movement and its agenda setting role in the 1906 Oklahoma Constitutional Convention Delegate Elections

---

[92] *See id.* § 2.

[93] *See id.* § 1.

[94] OKLA. STAT. ANN. Tit. 31(A)(5, 13) (2005), *compare with* OKLA. TERRITORY STAT. 2860 § 3 (1890).

[95]

The Organic Act itself was seen as precursor for statehood by many, with the issue remaining whether the Twin Territories would enter the union as one state or two. Many residents of Indian Territory opposed statehood under any circumstances, because they saw statehood as leading to the dissolution of their tribal governments and the loss of their treaty rights (the removal treaties guaranteed the tribes that their landholdings would never be incorporated into a state without their consent), while others saw separate statehood for Indian Territory as being the best method to preserve their separate way of life. At the same time, most residents of Oklahoma Territory[96] (as well as a significant number of the residents of Indian Territory[97]) favored single statehood.

In the midst of this debate in the Twin Territories, was another ongoing debate in

---

[96] VICTOR E. HARLOW, HARLOW'S OKLAHOMA HISTORY 248 (Arrell M. Gibson ed. Harlow Publishing Corp. 1967) (1934).
[97] AMOS D. MAXWELL, THE SEQUOYAH CONSTITUTIONAL CONVENTION 54-56 (Meador Publishing Company 1953

Washington, D.C. between Republicans and Democrats over the question of statehood for the remaining territories in the continental United States, Arizona, New Mexico, Oklahoma and Indian Territories. All of these territories were believed by the Republicans (including President Teddy Roosevelt) to in the future likely be states that would someday be dominated by the Democratic Party (with the resulting bump in the US Senate of 2 seats per state). As a result of this dynamic, Democrats argued for separate statehood for all four territories, while Republicans argued that only two states should be created from the territories, by combining Oklahoma and Indian Territories into one state, while Arizona and New Mexico territories would be merged into another single state.[98]

Due to the political dynamics of this debate, it seemed that single statehood was a more likely proposition, however the hurdle to this objective by the Single Statehood

---

[98] VICTOR E. HARLOW, HARLOW'S OKLAHOMA HISTORY 235-236 (Arell M. Gibson ed. Harlow Publishing Corp. 1967) (1934).

movement was the treaty rights of the five civilized tribes, which forbid their respective tribes from being incorporated within the bounds of any state, without the consent of the tribe itself.[99] However, pro-statehood forces were able to weaken the tribes' ability to preserve a separate place for Indian peoples (either outside any state, or within a separate Indian state in what is now Eastern Oklahoma) through two major forces: the forced allotments of land to individual tribal members (and the later dissolution of tribal governments) and secondly the Sequoyah statehood movement's failure to achieve its stated goals.[100]

The forced allotments of land to Indians was a central goal for those advocating single statehood since the practice of communal Indian land tenure prevented whites from purchasing land from individual Indians and served to stifle the

---

[99] 26 Stat. 81 § 1 & 2 (1890).
[100] VICTOR E. HARLOW, HARLOW'S OKLAHOMA HISTORY 252-253 (Arrell M. Gibson ed. Harlow Publishing Corp. 1967) (1934).

growth of individual capitalist interests in the territory. One example of this sentiment can be seen in this description of the Cherokee Nation by U.S. Senator H.L. Dawes:

> *The head chief told us that there was not a family in that whole nation that did not have a home of its own. There was not a pauper in that nation, and the nation did not owe a dollar. It built its own capitol . . ., and it built its schools and hospital. Yet the defect of the system was apparent. They have got as far as they can go, because they own their land in common. It is Henry George's system, and that that there is no enterprise to make your home better than that of your neighbors. There is no selfishness which is at the bottom of civilization.*[101]

---

[101] DANNEY GOBLE, PROGRESSIVE OKLAHOMA: THE MAKING OF A NEW KIND OF STATE 67 (University of Oklahoma Press 1980) *quoting* Angie Debo, AND

The pro-single statehood forces got their way when the Dawes General Allotment Act was amended in 1893 to provide that the citizens of the Five Civilized tribes would no longer hold their land in common, but instead would have individual title to their land.[102] In theory these new individual land titles were inalienable, but through a variety of means (which at this time was called "grafting") many of the Indian landowners were quickly deprived of their lands through either long-term leases or through outright alienation.[103]

SILL THE WATERS RUN: THE BETRAYAL OF THE FIVE CIVILIZED TRIBES 21-22 (Princeton University Press 1972) *also see Henry George* WIKIPEDIA (2005) *AVAILABLE AT:* http://en.wikipedia.org/wiki/Henry_George. Henry George was a well known but often discounted economist of that era.

[102] JIM BISSETT, AGRARIAN SOCIALISM IN AMERICA: MARX, JEFFERSON AND JESUS IN THE OKLAHOMA COUNTRYSIDE 1903-1920 18(University of Oklahoma Press 1999).

[103] *See generally* DANNEY GOBLE, PROGRESSIVE OKLAHOMA: THE MAKING OF A NEW KIND OF STATE 76-86 (University of Oklahoma Press 1980) *also see* JIM BISSETT, AGRARIAN SOCIALISM IN AMERICA:

The actual affect of the Dawes allotments was to dilute the influence and power of the Five Civilized Tribes in Indian Territory, which set the stage for the next significant development in the advent of the single-statehood movement: the Sequoyah Movement.[104] The Sequoyah Movement was developed by some members of the Indian Territory Democratic Party who were seeking to gain increased political power in the party[105], as well as to reduce resistance from the Five Civilized Tribes to eventual single-statehood (in fact an agreement was reached between the convention organizers and the Five Civilized Tribes, that the tribes would support single-statehood if the Sequoyah initiative failed[106]).

MARX, JEFFERSON AND JESUS IN THE OKLAHOMA COUNTRYSIDE 1903-1920 18(University of Oklahoma Press 1999).

[104]*Dawes Commission* WIKIPEDIA (2005) *AVAILABLE AT:* http://en.wikipedia.org/wiki/Dawes_Commission; *also see* DANNEY GOBLE, PROGRESSIVE OKLAHOMA: THE MAKING OF A NEW KIND OF STATE 72 (University of Oklahoma Press 1980).

[105]DANNEY GOBLE, PROGRESSIVE OKLAHOMA: THE MAKING OF A NEW KIND OF STATE 190 (University of Oklahoma Press 1980).

The initial call for a convention was made in early July 1905 (which received little attention) but a second call for a convention (this time endorsed by the chiefs of the Five Civilized Tribes after being persuaded by Charles N. Haskell that it was better for the tribes to participate in this convention than to not have a voice in the statehood movement[107]) was sent out on July 18 with a better reception.[108]

Then on August 8, 1905 local "conventions" were held in each of the twenty-six districts of Indian Territory to elect delegates to the Sequoyah convention.[109]

---

[106] *See id.* 190-191.

[107] VICTOR E. HARLOW, HARLOW'S OKLAHOMA HISTORY 250-251 (Arrell M. Gibson ed. Harlow Publishing Corp. 1967) (1934), *also see* AMOS D. MAXWELL, THE SEQUOYAH CONSTITUTIONAL CONVENTION 50-53 (Meador Publishing Company 1953).

[108] DANNEY GOBLE, PROGRESSIVE OKLAHOMA: THE MAKING OF A NEW KIND OF STATE 191 (University of Oklahoma Press 1980).

[109] DANNEY GOBLE, PROGRESSIVE OKLAHOMA: THE MAKING OF A NEW KIND OF STATE 191 (University of Oklahoma Press 1980), *also see* AMOS D. MAXWELL,

The Sequoyah convention began its meetings on August 21, 1905 in Muskogee[110] . The Convention's Chairman was the popular Creek Chief Pleasant Porter[111] but the actual political leadership of the convention came from five men[112] who would in time come to profit handsomely from the political move they made: Charles N. Haskell (who would later become the first Governor of the State of Oklahoma), William H. "Alfalfa Bill" Murray (who would later be the President of the Oklahoma Constitutional convention, was the architect of Oklahoma's early Jim Crow laws, and later serve as a notorious

---

THE SEQUOYAH CONSTITUTIONAL CONVENTION 54-60 (Meador Publishing Company 1953). I use the word "convention" loosely to refer to these local meetings, since many of these gatherings were in fact secret meetings that the general public was not invited to.

[110] AMOS D. MAXWELL, THE SEQUOYAH CONSTITUTIONAL CONVENTION 62 (Meador Publishing Company 1953).

[111] DANNEY GOBLE, PROGRESSIVE OKLAHOMA: THE MAKING OF A NEW KIND OF STATE 191-192 (University of Oklahoma Press 1980).

[112] See id.

governor during the early Great Depression[113]
), W.W. Hastings (who would later serve as
a US Congressman from Oklahoma[114]) John
R. Thomas (a U.S. Judge sitting in
Muskogee[115]) and Robert L. Owen (served
as Superintendent of the Five Civilized
Tribes[116] and later served as U.S. Senator for
Oklahoma from 1907-1925[117]).

The actual work of the Sequoyah
convention took place rapidly (the
convention adjourned on September 8,
1905), [118] and the constitution was ratified
by the voters of Indian Territory by a vote
of 56,279 to 9,073.[119]

---

[113] *William H. Murray* WIKIPEDIA (2005) *AVAILABLE
AT:* http://en.wikipedia.org/wiki/Alfalfa_bill_murray.

[114] VICTOR E. HARLOW, HARLOW'S OKLAHOMA
HISTORY 281 (Arrell M. Gibson ed. Harlow
Publishing Corp. 1967) (1934).

[115] *See id.* 246, 252.

[116] *See id.* 188.

[117] *See id.* 274, 305.

[118] AMOS D. MAXWELL, THE SEQUOYAH
CONSTITUTIONAL CONVENTION 62 (Meador
Publishing Company 1953).

[119] DANNEY GOBLE, PROGRESSIVE OKLAHOMA: THE
MAKING OF A NEW KIND OF STATE 193 (University of
Oklahoma Press 1980), *also see* AMOS D. MAXWELL,

The eventual exemption provisions of the Sequoyah constitution[120] were significant in that they enshrined the homestead and the personal property exemptions in the constitution itself (following the example of the Arkansas constitution), as well as setting a precedent in providing for generous homestead exemptions (interestingly though the rural homestead exemption was more limited than the current Indian Territory exemption that was derived from Arkansas statutes by way of the Organic Act).

Similar to the exemption provisions of the Oklahoma Territory, there were two separate sets of exemptions for heads of household and for non-heads of household (rejecting the Nebraska approach that was

THE SEQUOYAH CONSTITUTIONAL CONVENTION 102 (Meador Publishing Company 1953). Goble's work gives the vote count as 57,000 to 9,000, while Maxwell's work gives the vote count as 56,279 to 9,073, so I'm assuming that Goble rounded off the numbers which is why I've used Maxwell's numbers in the text.

[120] *See id. 622-675 quoting* SEQUOYAH CONST. (1906).

first used in Oklahoma Territory, while adopting the approach later adopted by the Oklahoma Territorial Legislative Assembly as well as the approach currently in place in Indian Territory by way of Arkansas law). Under the Sequoyah constitution, heads of household were entitled to the protection of a rural homestead of 100 acres with a value of up to $5000 in one or more parcels, or a homestead of 40 acres of any value. Urban homesteads were protected up to 1 acre with a value of up to $5000 or a ¼ acre of any value. Heads of household were also entitled the personal property exemptions that consisted of "$500 in specific articles or money," clothing, and $300 in tools of the trade and farm implements. Non-heads of household were not entitled to a homestead exemption, and the property exemption was limited to "$200 in specific articles of money"[121], clothing, and $300 in tools of the trade and farm implements.

---

[121] 1 THE STATE OF OKLAHOMA, THE OKLAHOMA RED BOOK 622-675 State of Oklahoma 1912 *quoting* SEQUOYAH CONST. (1906). The only copy of the Sequoyah convention that I have found gives this quote as "specific articles of money", but I believe this must be a typographical error, since the

The Sequoyah constitution also provided for a related provision that is not found in the eventual Oklahoma state constitution (but is found in the laws of the state of Texas, Pennsylvania and South Carolina today[122] in a modified form): a ban on wage garnishments for wages earned during the last two months.

While the Sequoyah Movement failed in receiving Congressional approval for single statehood[123] (which was likely never the goal of the leaders of the movement anyway[124]

---

corresponding exemption provision for heads of household says "specific articles or money." The context of the exemptions would seem to indicate that the text of "specific articles or money" makes more sense.

[122] *State Collection Laws* CARREON AND ASSOCIATES (1997, 2005) *AVAILABLE AT:*
http://www.carreonandassociates.com/articles/collectionlaws.htm

[123] DANNEY GOBLE, PROGRESSIVE OKLAHOMA: THE MAKING OF A NEW KIND OF STATE 193 (University of Oklahoma Press 1980).

[124] *Id.* at 193. "As an effort to realize separate statehood – certainly separate and distinctly *Indian* statehood – the Sequoyah movement was a failure if not a fraud."

) it did serve to push Congress to action on the statehood issue[125] and also gave Democrats in the Twin Territories a radical and populist platform on which to campaign for. The provisions of the Sequoyah constitution served as an impetus for two documents that would serve to elect a landslide of democrats to the Oklahoma Constitutional Convention: the "Shawnee Demands" of the combined labor movement of The Twin Territories[126] as well as the "suggested platform" for constitutional convention delegates that was adopted in July 1906[127] (this platform is

---

[125] *Oklahoma Enabling Act of 1906*

[126] Kenny L. Brown, *Progressivism in Oklahoma Politics, 1900-1913: A Reinterpretation*, "AN OKLAHOMA I HAD NEVER SEEN BEFORE": ALTERNATIVE VIEWS OF OKLAHOMA HISTORY 45 (Davis D. Joyce ed., University of Oklahoma Press 1994), *also see* DANNEY GOBLE, PROGRESSIVE OKLAHOMA: THE MAKING OF A NEW KIND OF STATE 228-229 (University of Oklahoma Press 1980). Those participating in the drafting of the "Shawnee Demands" included the Rail unions, the Twin Territories Federation of Labor, and the Oklahoma Farmers Union. Kate Bernard, the well-liked advocate for the oppressed was also present, representing the Women's International Union Labor League.

said to be "partially a commentary upon the wordy Sequoyah charter: nearly half of its substantive planks were taken from that constitution's provisions.")[128] For this context of this paper, these documents are significant as they both call for liberal homestead and exemption laws, with the "Shawnee Demands" stating that "We demand a liberal homestead and exemption,"[129] while the "Suggested Platform" states that "We favor liberal homestead and other exemption laws…"[130]

It was from the context of this populist movement (as manifested in the Sequoyah constitution and later political organizing) that the voters of the Twin Territories elected a landslide of Democrats to represent them at the Constitutional Convention (99 Democrats, 12 Republicans

---

[127] DANNEY GOBLE, PROGRESSIVE OKLAHOMA: THE MAKING OF A NEW KIND OF STATE 230-231 (University of Oklahoma Press 1980).

[128] *See id.* 196.

[129] *See id.* 228-229.

[130] *See id.* 230-231 *quoting "Suggestions for a Platform" for Democratic Party Oklahoma Constitutional Convention Delegate candidates* § 13.

and 1 Independent were elected to the convention).[131]

4. 1906-1907 – The Oklahoma Constitutional Convention's consideration of Homestead and Personal Property Exemption Laws

The drafting of the exemption provisions of the Oklahoma state convention consisted of four stages: (1) the submission of proposition and resolutions by convention delegates, (2) the consideration of the proposals by the Homestead and Exemption Committee and the drafting of Committee Report #37[132], (3) the reconvening of the Homestead and Exemption committee and the drafting of Resubmitted Committee Report #37[133], (4)

---

[131] DANNEY GOBLE, PROGRESSIVE OKLAHOMA: THE MAKING OF A NEW KIND OF STATE 200-201 (University of Oklahoma Press 1980).

[132] *Committee Report* #37, OKLA. CONST. CONVENTION (January 29, 1907) (Committee on Homesteads and Exemptions), *MICROFILMED ON:* Okla. Const. Convention tapes, Okla. Historical Society Library.

[133] *Committee* Report #37 *Recommitted*, OKLA.

the revision of Committee Report #37[134] and (5) the adoption of the final language by the convention as a whole. (To aid the reader in considering the valuations discussed in the various proposals and committee reports, see Appendix B for a table that shows the current valuation of 1906 dollars.)

There were seven propositions and resolutions submitted by convention delegates on the subject of exemptions (from what I can tell there was no procedural difference between a convention proposition and a convention resolution other than the perambulatory language, since both a proposition and a resolution functioned similar to how a bill functions in a legislative body). The primary difference in approach in the various proposals was whether the constitution's exemption

CONST. CONVENTION (February 12, 1907) (Committee on Homesteads and Exemptions), *MICROFILMED ON:* Okla. Const. Convention tapes, Okla. Historical Society Library.

[134] *Committee* Report #37, OKLA. CONST. CONVENTION (February 25, 1907) (Revision, Compilation, Style and Arrangement committee), *MICROFILMED ON:* Okla. Const. Convention tapes, Okla. Historical Society Library.

provisions would exempt the homestead only, personal property only, or both the homestead and personal property.

Four of the proposals provided for only homestead exemptions to be included in the constitution. Resolution #66 (introduced by Delegate Ellis)[135] provided for a scheme that is almost identical to the eventual exemption scheme adopted by the convention: a 160 acre rural exemption and a 1 acre urban exemption. This resolution also specifically cites Kansas as the source for its exemption amounts.[136]

The other three proposals that provided for a homestead but not personal property exemptions had a twist that resolution #66 did not provide, combining a monetary valuation cap to the acreage limit. Resolution #110 (introduced by Delegate Covey)[137] only applied the monetary cap to

---

[135] Proposition 66, Okla. Const. Convention (Dec. 3, 1906), *MICROFILMED ON:* Okla. Const. Convention tapes, Okla. Historical Society Library.

[136] *Id.* at 2.

[137] Res. 110, Okla. Const. Convention (Dec. 4, 1906),

urban homesteads (the rural homestead was 40 acres, while the urban homestead did not specify an acre limit but instead was limited to a $500 valuation.[138]), while resolutions #68 (introduced by Delegate Gardner, which provided for a rural exemption of 80 acres worth less than $5000 or 40 acres of any value and an urban exemption of 1 acre worth less than $5000 or ¼ acre of any value [139]

MICROFILMED ON: Okla. Const. Convention tapes, Okla. Historical Society Library.

[138] Res. 110, Okla. Const. Convention (Dec. 4, 1906), *MICROFILMED ON:* Okla. Const. Convention tapes, Okla. Historical Society Library. This resolution also provided for a early form of "social security" in which the probate judge and county commissioners are charged with renting out the homesteads of persons who are unable to derive income from their lands (with the funds being paid into the county's general school fund), while the county is response to provide "a suitable nurse, food and clothing for said owner, until his disability shall be removed from death or recovery." Of course knowing the history of Grafting and other crooked maneuvers to take away people's land in that era, it is understandable why this easily-abused provision was not included by the committee in its first draft of the Exemption provisions.

[139] Res. 68, Okla. Const. Convention (Dec. 3, 1906), *MICROFILMED ON:* Okla. Const. Convention tapes, Okla. Historical Society Library.

) and resolution #172 (introduced by Delegate Carr, which provided for a rural homestead of 100 acres with a value of up to $3000 or 40 acres of any value, and an urban homestead worth less than $3000[140])

Two of the proposals provided for a very limited set of exemptions that covered only personal property exemptions. Resolution #49 (introduced by Delegate Graham) provided an exemption for clothing with no limit of value as well as additional personal property with a cap of $200 for non-heads of household and $500 for heads-of household.[141] Resolution #318 (introduced by Delegate Ellis) was even stingier, providing only for a $200 personal property exemption for heads of household.[142]

---

[140] Res. 172, Okla. Const. Convention (Dec. 5, 1906), *MICROFILMED ON:* Okla. Const. Convention tapes, Okla. Historical Society Library.

[141] Res. 49, Okla. Const. Convention (Dec. 1, 1906), *MICROFILMED ON:* Okla. Const. Convention tapes, Okla. Historical Society Library.

[142] Proposition 318, Okla. Const. Convention (Dec. 12, 1906), *MICROFILMED ON:* Okla. Const. Convention tapes, Okla. Historical Society Library.

Finally, one of the resolutions followed the direction set by the Sequoyah constitution in providing for the delineation of both homestead and personal property exemptions in the constitution itself. Proposition #149 (introduced by Delegate Swarts) provided for an exemption of $200 of personal property for non-head of households, with a more comprehensive set of exemptions for heads of households: $1500 homestead, an unlimited value of clothing, books, farm implements and tools of the trade, and an additional $500 in personal property.[143]

The committee in its first report (dated January 29, 1907, signed by the committee members and committee chairman Neal B. Gardener,)[144] drafted an exemption provision that provided for both the

---

[143] Proposition 149, Okla. Const. Convention (Dec. 4, 1906), *MICROFILMED ON:* Okla. Const. Convention tapes, Okla. Historical Society Library.

[144] *Committee Report* #37, OKLA. CONST. CONVENTION (January 29, 1907) (Committee on Homesteads and Exemptions), *MICROFILMED ON:* Okla. Const. Convention tapes, Okla. Historical Society Library.

homestead and the personal property exemptions to be included in the constitution, which was the same approach adopted by the Sequoyah Convention (and previously the Arkansas Constitution of 1874). The personal property provisions provided that only clothing for resident non-heads of family would be exempt[145] while resident heads of families and married couples would be entitled to an exemption for the family's clothing and $500 worth of additional personal property.[146]

The record of the convention does not provide for the story behind the story but the Homestead and Exemptions committee met again (this time with J.C. Graham signing the committee report as "Chairman Pro Tem" of the committee[147]) and drafted a revised version of the provision, this time removing the personal property exemptions

---

[145] *Id.* at 1.

[146] *Id.* at 1-2.

[147] *Committee* Report #37 *Recommitted*, OKLA. CONST. CONVENTION (February 12, 1907) (Committee on Homesteads and Exemptions), *MICROFILMED ON:* Okla. Const. Convention tapes, Okla. Historical Society Library.

of the prior committee report and instead place into effect sections 1, 3, 6 and 7 of the Oklahoma Territorial Exemption laws.[148] This "Re-committed" version of Committee Report #37 was presented to the body on February 12, 1907.[149]

Then on February 25, 1907[150] the Revision, Compilation, Style and Arrangement committee published its version of Committee Report #37[151] which is almost identical to the final version that was adopted by the body as a whole. This version differs from the second version of

---

[148] *See id.*, *citing* OKLA. TERRITORY STAT., 2985 § 1, 3, 6, 7 (1903). The references to the Territorial exemption law reference the exemptions for heads of household, non heads of family, and some exceptions to these exemptions.

[149] *Committee* Report #37 *Recommitted*, OKLA. CONST. CONVENTION (February 12, 1907) (Committee on Homesteads and Exemptions), 4 *MICROFILMED ON:* Okla. Const. Convention tapes, Okla. Historical Society Library.

[150] *Committee* Report #37, OKLA. CONST. CONVENTION (February 25, 1907) (Revision, Compilation, Style and Arrangement committee), *MICROFILMED ON:* Okla. Const. Convention tapes, Okla. Historical Society Library.

[151] *See id.*

Committee Report #37, in that it omits the personal property provisions all together but does provide references to Oklahoma Territorial statutes that are to no longer be in force after the adoption of the Constitution.[152]

The final version of the Homestead Exemption provision that was adopted by the Convention[153] was identical to the third version of Committee Report #37, except that the phrase "Nothing in this Constitution shall prevent or prohibit any person from mortgaging or encumbering his personal exemptions" was inserted.[154]

---

[152] OKLA. TERR. STAT. Ch. 34 Sec. 4&3, 5 (1893). The statutory provisions referenced refer to an exception ion to the homestead exemption for mortgaged indebtedness for improvements and an exception to exemptions on personal property in the case of a landlord who is enforcing a statutory lien.

[153] OKLA. CONST. art. 12 (1907) (amended 1997).

[154] See Committee Report #37, OKLA. CONST. CONVENTION (February 25, 1907) (Revision, Compilation, Style and Arrangement committee), MICROFILMED ON: Okla. Const. Convention tapes, Okla. Historical Society Library. This line was inserted between lines 2 and 3 of committee report 3rd. See also OKLA. CONST. Art. XII § 3.

The Oklahoma State Constitution was approved by the people of Oklahoma in the election of September 17, 1907 (winning approval by 71% of voters)[155], and was approved by President Theodore Roosevelt on November 16, 1907 despite his stated opinion that the constitution was "not fit for publication"[156]

5. The 1997 Constitutional Amendment

Since 1907 there has been only one amendment to the Homestead Provision (enacted in 1997).[157] This amendment made two major changes to the Homestead Exemption Law; the first change being that it protected rural homesteads from being subjected to the much lower urban

---

[155] DANNEY GOBLE, PROGRESSIVE OKLAHOMA: THE MAKING OF A NEW KIND OF STATE 225 (University of Oklahoma Press 1980).

[156] *Id.* at 226, 203. President Roosevelt's low opinion of the Oklahoma Constitution is not surprising since he referred to the convention delegates as "a zoological garden of cranks."

[157] OKLA. CONST. art. 12 § 1 (2005), *also see* OKLA. STAT. ANN. Tit. 31 § 2 (2005). The identical homestead provisions of the Constitution and statute were both amended.

homestead limitation, if the homestead was located within territory annexed by a city or town after November 1, 1997.[158] This protection is important to holders of many homesteads, since many Oklahoma communities in recent years have preemptively annexed large portions of surrounding rural areas to fend off an annexation effort by another neighboring community,[159] which prior to this amendment would effectively shrink the protected acreage of landowners residing in this newly annexed territory.

The second major change of the 1997 amendment to the Homestead Exemption was that it altered the rules for urban homesteads. Prior to this amendment, urban homesteads were limited to 1 acre in

---

[158] *See* OKLA. CONST. art. 12 § 1(B) (2005), *also see* OKLA. STAT. ANN. Tit. 31 § 2 (2005).

[159] *B'ville's boom in annexations continues as 80 acres added*, Tulsa World September 11, 2005, *available on Westlaw at:* 2005 WLNR 14360549. This one example of the rapid acceleration in annexation by urban and suburban communities of areas that once could have constituted rural homesteads under Oklahoma law.

size that was worth less than $5,000, or up to ¼ of any value.[160] The new version of the Homestead exemption protected all non-business urban homesteads of 1 acre of any value, but added a $5,000 valuation cap on any urban homestead in which more than 25% of the square footage of the homestead improvements were used for business purposes.[161]

B. Exemption provisions found in statutes

Oklahoma's statutory property exemptions[162] have been since day one (actually prior to day one, considering the similarities between the current state statutes and the exemption statutes of Oklahoma Territory[163]) provided an interesting assortment of personal property exemptions that seek to satisfy differing and sometimes competing

---

[160] OKLA. CONST. art. 12 § 1 (1907) (amended 1997).

[161] OKLA. CONST. art. 12 § 1 (2005).

[162] OKLA. STAT. ANN. Tit. 31 (2005).

[163] OKLA. TERRITORY STAT., 2860 (1890).

interests. Upon statehood, the prior exemption statutes of Oklahoma Territory were carried forward into applicability since they were "not repugnant to this Constitution,"[164] and interestingly enough remain law today with a few significant changes: (1) the eligibility of residents who are not heads of family to enjoy property exemptions, (2) the change of the transportation-related exemptions to reflect that fact that most people today travel by automobiles and not by horse-drawn conveyances, (3) the placing of dollar limitation caps on some categories of property, and (4) the addition of exemptions to cover modern methods of saving for retirement.[165]

The most recent amendment to the property exemptions found in Oklahoma statutes went into effect on August 26, 2005.[166] This amendment made the following changes to

---

[164] OKLA. CONST. SCHED. § 2 (2005).

[165] *Compare* OKLA. STAT. 34 § 3342 (1910) *and* OKLA. STAT. ANN. Tit. 31(2005).

[166] OKLA. CONST. art. 12 § 1 (2005), *compare with* OKLA. CONST. art. 12 § 1 (1907) (amended 1997).

the prior personal property exemptions: (1) a specific reference to a "personal computer and related equipment" was added to the household goods and furnishings exemption,[167] (2) the dollar limitation cap for tools of the trade and farm implements was raised from \$5,000 to \$10,000,[168] (3) the motor vehicle exemption was raised from \$3,000 to \$7,500, (4) a \$3,000 exemption was added for wedding and anniversary rings, (5) and the gun exemption (which previously just exempted "one gun") was rewritten to read as:

Guns, not to exceed Two Thousand Dollars (\$2,000.00) in aggregate value, that are held primarily for the personal, family or household use of such person or a dependent of such person, provided that nothing in this subsection shall be construed to allow a person to exempt guns which are used mainly as an investment or nonpersonal, family or household use;[169]

---

[167] OKLA. CONST. art. 12 § 1 (3) (2005).

[168] *See id.* at (5).

[169] *See id.* at (14).

Based on the choices that the legislature has made in both drafting and revising the original exemption statutes, it does appear that the legislature intended to protect the debtor (and the debtor's family) family in some significant ways, by exempting (at least to some degree) the debtor's home, means of transportation, clothing and personal effects, means of making a living, and provisions for retirement. The legislature also appears to be willing to periodically adjust the specific protected interests (i.e. recognizing society's changed mode of ordinary transportation) but has retained a significant amount of respect for the original pro-debtor principles found in the current law's roots.

C. Key Interpretive Case Law

While bankruptcy law is primarily an issue of federal law, exemptions in bankruptcy are found in state law, so the decisions of both federal bankruptcy (and other federal courts on appeal) and state courts play another important role in creating the exemption law. In this section I will take a non-exhaustive look at some of the key refinements that interpretative case law has made on the Oklahoma property exemptions.

1. The Homestead Exemption as interpreted by case law

Under Oklahoma law, the central issue that is at stake in determining if a homestead exists is look for intention for the land to be a homestead coupled with actual usage of the land as a homestead. The central case on this point is the 1923 Oklahoma Supreme Court case of Kerns v. Warden.[170] The Kerns decision holds that:

> (U)nder the provisions of the Oklahoma Constitution and statute as construed by this court, the homestead character of the land is . . . (determined with) two requisites (that) must concur as to such portion:: (1)

[170] Kerns v. Warden, 213 P. 70, 72 (OKLA. 1923).

The owner must intend the property as a part of his homestead; and (2) he must in some way use it as such. Where the land owned does not exceed 160 acres, and a portion thereof is not used in any way as a homestead, and where the owner does not evince by overt acts an intention to immediately use the same as such, such portion of the 160 acres will not be considered a part of the homestead. As to whether such property is a homestead is a question of fact to be determined by the evidence.

At the same time, once a homestead character has attached to a piece of land, it is not considered to be abandoned by a temporary absence of the owner, but rather "there must be an intention at the time of going away, or an intention formed after removal, never to return, the intent of the parties being the controlling fact."[171]

Another issue that arises in the rural homestead context is whether a rural Homestead can consist of more than one tract of land, and if so what does it take to impress a homestead character upon multiple detached tracts? The homestead provisions of the Oklahoma Constitution provide that a rural homestead "shall consist of not more than one hundred and sixty acres of land, which may be in one or more parcels, to be selected by the owner," but leaves unanswered the exact parameters of this law.

Of the many cases that address this point[172], probably the best one to fully explain the law on this topic is the 1923 Oklahoma Supreme Court case of Williams v. Watkins.[173]

---

[171] German State Bank of Elk City v. Ptachek, 169 P. 1094 (OKLA. 1918).

[172] *See* Mitchell v. Quinton, 116 P2d 995 (OKLA. 1941), Powell v. Powell , 116 P2d 889 (OKLA. 1941), Exchange Nat. Bank of Tulsa v. Rose, 103 P.2d 496 (OKLA. 1940), Cooper v. Long, 220 P. 610 (OKLA. 1923), Watson v. Manning, 156 P. 184 (OKLA. 1916), Gooch v. Gooch, 133 P. 242 (OKLA. 1913).

[173] Williams v. Watkins, 219 P. 643 (OKLA. 1923).

In the Williams decision, the court explains that Oklahoma (both in Western Oklahoma with its history of homesteading and in Eastern Oklahoma with its history of allotments of small tracts of land to the original Indian owners) has a unique history with regards to land ownership in which farmers desiring to farm more than a small tract of land by the time of statehood often had to purchase multiple tracts from various owners, often scattered over a broad geographic area. The court argues that this is why the Oklahoma Constitutional Convention chose to allow heads of families to designate multiple tracts of land as a single homestead (up to a total of 160 acres), rejecting the prior Oklahoma Territory statutory precedent which allowed for a homestead consisting of only one tract of land.[174] The court went on to explain that while only one tract of land may be "occupied" at one time[175], that other tracts of land can be "selected" (to use the Constitutional language) through if the owner's express intention is to "use the

---

[174] *Id.* at 644-645.

[175] *Id.* at 645-646.

other tract or tracts in the interest of the homestead,"[176] and that there be "open evidence of this intention as will prevent the use of this right as a shield for fraud."[177]

2. Personal Property Exemption as interpreted by case law

Due to Oklahoma's "laundry list" approach to its personal property exemptions, there have been a significant number of cases that have discussed the various aspects of the exemptions and whether a particular item of personal property fits under a specified category found in statute. The extent of much of this case law goes beyond the scope of this paper, but I will discuss briefly a few of the significant cases that also happen to elucidate upon the general principles that the courts use in interpreting Oklahoma's personal property exemptions.

---

[176] *Id.* at 646.

[177] *Id.* at 646), *quoting* Illinois Life Insurance Co. v. Rogers, 160 P. 56 (1916), *quoting* Foley v. Holtkam, 66 SW 891 (1902).

With regards to the general approach that Oklahoma uses in interpreting its property exemptions, the Oklahoma Supreme Court in 1915 adopted the rule of the Oklahoma Territorial Courts which provided that "Exemption laws should be liberally construed; and, where there is a doubt as to whether certain property is exempt or not, the doubt should be resolved in favor of the exemption."[178] This rule has been frequently discussed since[179], including in a 2003 10th Circuit BAP (Bankruptcy Appellate Panel) decision.[180]

In examination of specific exemption provisions, a few cases are instructive not only for their value in interpreting a particular provision but also as being an

---

[178] Phelan v. Lacey, 151 P. 1070, (OKLA. 1915), *citing* Nelson v. Fightmaster, 44 P. 213, (OKLA.TERR. 1896).

[179] *see In re* Allen§s Guardianship, 78 P.2d 700, 701, (OKLA. 1938); Field v. Goat, 173 P. 364, 364, (OKLA. 1918); *In re* Walker, 139 B.R. 31, 34 (N.D.OKLA. 1990); *In re Payne, 215 B.R. 889, 891,* (BANKR.N.D.OKLA. 1997*); In re* Fisher, 11 B.R. 666, 668 (BANKR.W.D.OKLA. Jun 11, 1981).

[180] *In re* Robinson, 295 B.R. 147 (B.A.P. 10TH CIR. 2003)

example of the general approach the courts take in interpreting the Oklahoma exemptions.

One such case deals with the issue of the Tools of the Trade exemption. In the case of In re Johnson, the debtor's pickup was deemed to be a "tool of the trade" since the debtor's livelihood was rural mail delivery and the debtor owned no other working vehicle that could perform this task,[181] which illustrates the "problem-solving" approach that courts interpreting the Oklahoma property exemptions tend to use, which I think is the result of the tone that the legislature sets in drafting generous personal property exemptions.[182]

However despite the latitude that courts often seem to use in interpreting the Oklahoma property exemptions, there are

---

[181] *In re* Johnson, 101 B.R. 280,281-282 (BANKR. W.D. OKLA. 1989).

[182] *see generally* In re Mackey, 209 B.R. 251, 252 (BANKR. E.D. OKLA. 1997), Lindsey v. Kingfisher Bank 832 P.2d 1, 4 (OKLA. 1992), In re Siegmann 757 P.2d 820, 822 (OKLA. 1988).

also cases in which the court seems to rely on a technical interpretation of the exemptions that is focused on the specific intent of the legislature rather the more broad general purposes of the statute. Two examples of this trend both deal with livestock. In the case of In re Wilford, the court held that the debtors did not hold an exemption in hogs since the debtors raised hogs for profit and not for "personal, family or household use," [183] while in the case of In re Luckinbill held that a debtor's five Hereford cows and calves were not exempt since the Hereford breed of cattle is bred for beef production and not milk production.[184] Interestingly the courts in both cases seem to focus on the narrow historical construction of the law (that a farm family in statehood days would raise much of its own food and supplies) instead of recognizing the reality of most modern farm operations (in which a farm family sells

---

[183] *In re* Wiford, 105 B.R. 992, 1000 (BANKR. N.D. OKLA. 1989).

[184] *In re* Luckinbill, 163 B.R. 856 (W.D. OKLA. 1994).

products for market and then uses the proceeds to purchase food and other basic supplies).

As a whole it would seem that the Oklahoma personal property exemptions are "liberally construed," but only with regard to those exemptions that lack specificity, and that personal property exemptions are also often interpreted in a wooden way that seems contrary to the more broad purposes intended by the legislature. One could also argue that the legislative intent of the drafters of these exemption was to intentionally create this tension between liberal and conservative construction of the statute, which tends to result in a problem-solving fact-oriented approach to the case law.

Chapter 2 – The Functionality of Oklahoma's Current Property Exemption Laws

Do the current Oklahoma Exemption laws actually serve the interest that was intended to be set by the Oklahoma Constitutional convention and subsequent state legislatures? - This is not an easy question to answer because it requires us to not only examine the legislative intent of the Oklahoma exemption scheme, but also to consider two other questions: did the exemptions as drafted actually fulfill these purposes, and are the exemptions fulfilling those purposes today?

A. The past

This section will discuss the pre and post-statehood economic developments, including the Agricultural crisis of cotton farmers in the first decades (being crunched between low prices and high costs for credit and supplies), the dust bowl experience, the move to a post-agricultural economy, and how the negative impacts of these economic factors on Oklahomans were (or were not) alleviated by the exemption laws.

Oklahoma's economy during the era of the latter part of the era of The Twin Territories was based heavily on agriculture, but the methods varied greatly by region. Farmers in Oklahoma Territory primarily raised wheat with some corn, cotton and often livestock, while Farmers in Eastern Oklahoma tended to be tenant farmer who grew cotton, since most of the land was bought up by land speculators at the time of the Dawes allotments and tribal dissolution.[185] In both territories these tenant farmers were victims of a cruel system that attacked their means to thrive at both the production and consumption ends. They were exploited

---

[185] JIM BISSETT, AGRARIAN SOCIALISM IN AMERICA: MARX, JEFFERSON AND JESUS IN THE OKLAHOMA COUNTRYSIDE 1903-1920 18-19 (University of Oklahoma Press 1999).

when they brought their crops (particularly cotton) to town to sell since most other farmers brought their crops in at the same time resulting in a buyers market, while at the same time being exploited when they used the proceeds of their crop sales to buy supplies from local merchants who charged high prices, and mostly their were exploited through predatory lending practices (farmers during hard time often had to consent to a crop lien to secure credit and then had to pay a higher "credit price" for the supplies they needed.)[186]

This system resulted in a spiral of increasing debt and the resulting loss of the land by the actual "tillers of the earth"[187], to

---

[186] JIM BISSETT, AGRARIAN SOCIALISM IN AMERICA: MARX, JEFFERSON AND JESUS IN THE OKLAHOMA COUNTRYSIDE 1903-1920 15 (University of Oklahoma Press 1999).

[187] *See generally* JIM BISSETT, AGRARIAN SOCIALISM IN AMERICA: MARX, JEFFERSON AND JESUS IN THE OKLAHOMA COUNTRYSIDE 1903-1920 40-57 (University of Oklahoma Press 1999), *also see* DANNEY GOBLE, PROGRESSIVE OKLAHOMA: THE MAKING OF A NEW KIND OF STATE 163 (University of Oklahoma Press 1980). This crisis also played out in the inner workings of the Indiahoma Farmers Union,

such an extent that number of tenant farmers in Oklahoma increased from 43.7% in 1900 to 61.2% in 1935[188]

Given this steady drop in the rates of land ownership by farmers (which was in continuing existence before even statehood), one has to ask whether the Homestead and personal property exemptions were designed to protect family farmers or whether the protection was actually designed to protect absentee farmers? And if one does assume that this protection was designed to protect all farmers, then the next question is whether exemptions actually functioned to fulfill this purpose?

These questions are not easy to answer. The framers of the Oklahoma Constitution were

---

which at first was a strong advocate for working farmers but later was co-opted and finally destroyed by absentee farmers who did not till the earth themselves.

[188] JIM BISSETT, AGRARIAN SOCIALISM IN AMERICA: MARX, JEFFERSON AND JESUS IN THE OKLAHOMA COUNTRYSIDE 1903-1920 11 (University of Oklahoma Press 1999) *citing* John H. Souther, *Farm Tenancy in Oklahoma*, AGRICULTURAL EXTENSION STATION BULLETIN 7 (Dec. 1939).

folks who were quick to spout off platitudes in support of the working man[189], but in actuality many of those same delegates (most notably Convention President Alfalfa B. Murray) were actually large landholders[190], many of whom were responsible for the destruction of the Indiahoma Farmers Union out of frustration with the success that the so-called "dirt farmers" were making in organizing tenant farmers in

---

[189] IRVIN HURST, THE 46TH STAR: A HISTORY OF OKLAHOMA'S CONSTITUTIONAL CONVENTION AND EARLY STATEHOOD 6-7 (Western Heritage Books 1980) (1957), One notable example being Alfalfa Bill Murray's opening speech to the Oklahoma Constitutional Convention in which he spoke against interests buying up large amounts of real estate, in favor of the 8-hour work day and the evils of corruption by way of the "free pass."

[190] see JIM BISSETT, AGRARIAN SOCIALISM IN AMERICA: MARX, JEFFERSON AND JESUS IN THE OKLAHOMA COUNTRYSIDE 1903-1920 26 (University of Oklahoma Press 1999), also see DANNEY GOBLE, PROGRESSIVE OKLAHOMA: THE MAKING OF A NEW KIND OF STATE 191 (University of Oklahoma Press 1980). Alfalfa Bill Murray's statements against holding of large land interests by the rich is ironic given the fact that Murray himself was a wealthy landowner who had come to dominate the Chickasaw Nation by means of his political maneuvering as an inter-married citizen.

collective action against the oppressive class through the union.[191] It is true that the homestead exemption law did protect all landowners from involuntary liens on their homesteads, the problem was that for most poor farmers the real danger was not of an involuntary lien (since credit was unavailable unless you had collateral to secure it with) but of voluntary liens against one's crops and against one's land that were economically necessary to make it during hard times. If the legislature's intention was to protect all farmers of all economic classes, then the exemptions were a failure, at least during the early decades of Oklahoma history, because they did not protect farmers from the most serious economic pressures of that era.

---

[191] *See* DANNEY GOBLE, PROGRESSIVE OKLAHOMA: THE MAKING OF A NEW KIND OF STATE 162-163 (University of Oklahoma Press 1980), *also see* JIM BISSETT, AGRARIAN SOCIALISM IN AMERICA: MARX, JEFFERSON AND JESUS IN THE OKLAHOMA COUNTRYSIDE 1903-1920 51-57 (University of Oklahoma Press 1999).

B. The present - A look at how Oklahoma's Exemption laws function as compared to those of other states

Oklahoma faced a tremendous amount of economic and social turmoil in its early decades as a state: including the alienation of much of the land base of the Five Civilized Tribal members and freedmen[192], the agricultural crisis of the early part of this century[193], the turmoil of the xenophobic World War I era in Oklahoma (which included the defeat of the Green Corn Rebellion, the crushing of the Socialist

---

[192] *See generally* DANNEY GOBLE, PROGRESSIVE OKLAHOMA: THE MAKING OF A NEW KIND OF STATE 76-86 (University of Oklahoma Press 1980) *also see* JIM BISSETT, AGRARIAN SOCIALISM IN AMERICA: MARX, JEFFERSON AND JESUS IN THE OKLAHOMA COUNTRYSIDE 1903-1920 18(University of Oklahoma Press 1999).

[193] *See generally* JIM BISSETT, AGRARIAN SOCIALISM IN AMERICA: MARX, JEFFERSON AND JESUS IN THE OKLAHOMA COUNTRYSIDE 1903-1920 9-16 (University of Oklahoma Press 1999), *also see* DANNEY GOBLE, PROGRESSIVE OKLAHOMA: THE MAKING OF A NEW KIND OF STATE 153-158 (University of Oklahoma Press 1980).

Party, the persecution of pacifists, and the rise of the Ku Klux Klan)[194], the Tulsa race riot of 1921[195] and the frequent lynchings of African-Americans in the 1920's[196], and the cataclysmic days of the Great Depression and the Dust Bowl.[197] Given these extreme

---

[194] *See* generally JIM BISSETT, AGRARIAN SOCIALISM IN AMERICA: MARX, JEFFERSON AND JESUS IN THE OKLAHOMA COUNTRYSIDE 1903-1920 146-163 (University of Oklahoma Press 1999), *also see* VICTOR E. HARLOW, HARLOW'S OKLAHOMA HISTORY 284-287 (Arrell M. Gibson ed. Harlow Publishing Corp. 1967) (1934), Marvin E. Kroeker *"In Death You Shall Not Wear It Either": The Persecution of Mennonite Pacifists in Oklahoma*, "AN OKLAHOMA I HAD NEVER SEEN BEFORE": ALTERNATIVE VIEWS OF OKLAHOMA HISTORY 45 (Davis D. Joyce ed., University of Oklahoma Press 1994), *and* ROXANNE DUNBAR-ORTIZ, RED DIRT: GROWING UP OKIE 9-19 (Verso 1997).

[195] *Tulsa Race Riot*, OKLA. COMMISSION TO STUDY THE TULSA RACE RIOT OF 1921 (February 28, 2001) (Commission to Study the Tulsa Race Riot of 1921), *AVAILABLE AT:* http://www.ok-history.mus.ok.us/trrc/freport.htm.

[196] *See* Jimmie L. White, Jr. *James Brooks Ayers Robertson, 1919-1923*, OKLAHOMA'S GOVERNORS, 1907-1929: TURBULENT POLITICS 106-107 (LeRoy H. Fischer ed., Oklahoma Historical Society 1981).

[197] *See generally* JOHN STEINBECK, THE GRAPES OF WRATH (Viking Compass 1971) (1939), *also see* ROXANNE DUNBAR-ORTIZ, RED DIRT: GROWING UP

circumstances, one could argue that the inefficacy of the exemptions to protect desperate debtors from exploitation by abusive creditors was the result of the extreme situations of the day, and that the exemptions might actually function in fulfilling the state's desired intentions adequately today in a way that was impossible in the past.

To answer this question, I have chosen to compare the present-day functionality of the Oklahoma property exemptions with those of two other states, chosen for comparison purposes as being states representative of the common approaches used by other states. Oklahoma provides for

---

OKIE 21-36 (Verso 1997). *The Grapes of Wrath* gives a fictional version of what an Okie family might have went through during those days, while the chapter in *Red Dirt* referenced here discusses how the Great Depression affect one family who stayed put during that time and how those affects lingered long past the supposed end of the era. For criticism of the accuracy of *The Grapes of Wrath*, *see* Keith Windschuttle, *Steinbeck§s myth of the Okies*, NEW CRITERION (June 2002) *AVAILABLE AT:* http://www.newcriterion.com/archive/20/jun02/steinb eck.htm.

one of the more generous sets of property exemptions (the only states that have similar homestead exemption provisions are Florida[198], Iowa[199], Kansas[200], South Dakota[201], Texas[202], and the District of Columbia[203]), so in comparison I chose to look at the exemptions of Alaska (which was chosen as being a state that took a moderate approach to the homestead exemption while preserving generous personal property exemptions)[204], and New

---

[198] FLA. CONST. Art. 10 § 4.

[199] IOWA CODE ANN. § 561 (2005).

[200] KAN. STAT. ANN. § 60-2301 (2005).

[201] S.D. CODIFIED LAWS § 43-31-4 (2005).

[202] TEX. CONST. Art. 16, § 51.

[203] D.C. CODE ANN. § 15-501 (14) (2005).

[204] *See* Thomas G. W. Telfer, *Preliminary Paper on the Law of Personal Exemptions from Seizure* UNIFORM LAW CONFERENCE OF CANADA 2004 ANNUAL MEETING COMMERCIAL LAW DOCUMENTS, (2004) *AVAILABLE AT:*

http://www.ulcc.ca/en/poam2/CLS2004_Personal_Ex emptions_Paper_En.pdf, *also see* P.S. Deloria & Robert Laurence, *Negotiating Tribal-State Full Faith and Credit Agreements: The Topology of the Negotiation and the Merits of the Question*, 28 GA. L. REV. 365, 449 (1994), Lawrence Ponoroff, EXEMPTION LIMITATIONS: A TALE OF TWO

Jersey (chosen for being an aggressively anti-debtor state, but also one that allows for the use of the federal bankruptcy exemptions instead of its own repressive exemption scheme).[205]

1. In Comparison: A look at the exemption laws of Alaska and New Jersey

The source of law for Alaska's bankruptcy exemptions is in statues and case law (there are no exemption provisions in the Alaska constitution). Most of the key exemption provisions were created under the Alaska Exemptions Act (that is codified as chapter 38 of the Alaska Code of Civil Procedure[206]), which interestingly (as of 2005) is the only

---

SOLUTIONS 71 Am. Bankr. L.J. 221, 225 (1997).

[205] *See* William Houston Brown, Lawrence R. Ahern, III, & Nancy Fraas MacLean, BANKRUPTCY EXEMPTION MANUAL § 3.02 (2005 ed.) *AVAILABLE AT WESTLAW.* New Jersey's harsh exemption scheme is moderated by the state's "opting-in" of the federal bankruptcy exemptions, which allows New Jersey debtors to use either the state or federal bankruptcy exemptions.

[206] ALASKA STAT. § 09 (2005), *Also see* ALASKA ADMIN. CODE Tit. 8, § 95.030 (2005).

state exemption law to be based upon the Uniform Exemption Act.[207]

The source of law for New Jersey bankruptcy exemptions is found in statutes and case law, but in a practical sense the "real" New Jersey bankruptcy exemptions are found in the federal bankruptcy code since few debtors actually use the New Jersey bankruptcy exemptions.[208]

---

[207] *See* Thomas G. W. Telfer, *Preliminary Paper on the Law of Personal Exemptions from Seizure* UNIFORM LAW CONFERENCE OF CANADA 2004 ANNUAL MEETING COMMERCIAL LAW DOCUMENTS, (2004) *AVAILABLE AT:* http://www.ulcc.ca/en/poam2/CLS2004_Personal_Ex emptions_Paper_En.pdf, *also see* P.S. Deloria & Robert Laurence, *Negotiating Tribal-State Full Faith and Credit Agreements: The Topology of the Negotiation and the Merits of the Question*, 28 GA. L. REV. 365, 449 (1994), Lawrence Ponoroff, EXEMPTION LIMITATIONS: A TALE OF TWO SOLUTIONS 71 Am. Bankr. L.J. 221, 225 (1997).

[208] *See* John D. Kovac *Bankruptcy (Chapter 7) Article* WEBSITE FOR LAW OFFICE OF JOHN D. KOVAC (2000-2002) available at: http://www.kovaclaw.com/bankruptcy.html#4. "The State of New Jersey also offers exemptions, but these are far less useful than the federal exemptions and are rarely used."

The federal exemptions (most commonly used in New Jersey) actually are interestingly similar to the Alaska exemptions mentioned above because of the influence of the Uniform Exemption Act upon the federal bankruptcy exemptions.[209]

As compared to the exemption laws of Alaska and New Jersey (both state and federal exemptions), Oklahoma has a far more generous set of exemptions. For instance, Oklahoma debtors have a protected 160 acre rural homestead or a 1 acre urban homestead, with no valuation cape, while Alaska debtors are limited to a homestead with a dollar cap of $70,200 [210] that is adjusted periodically for inflation[211] and New Jersey debtors have a choice between a federal homestead exemption of $21,625[212] or a non-existent state homestead exemption.

[209] *See Matter of* Taff 10 B.R. 101, 105-106 (Bankr. Conn. 1981).

[210] ALASKA STAT. § 09.38.010 (2005), *Also see* ALASKA ADMIN. CODE Tit. 8, § 95.030 (2008).

[211] ALASKA STAT. § 7 09.38.015 (2005), *Also see* ALASKA ADMIN. CODE Tit. 8, § 95.030 (2008).

With regards to personal property, Oklahoma takes a detailed but generous approach, Alaska takes a more moderated approach (with lower valuation caps than Oklahoma uses in most cases), New Jersey takes a very limited approach under state law but provides for a moderated approach under the federal exemptions that is fairly similar to the approach used by Alaska. [213]

2. In Comparison: A look at how hypothetical debtors would be treated under the exemption laws of Oklahoma, Alaska and New Jersey

With this rudimentary understanding of the key property exemptions in Oklahoma, Alaska and New Jersey in place, we now turn to looking at how a hypothetical debtor(s) would fare under each state's exemption scheme in a chapter 7[214]. Five of

---

[212] 11 U.S.C.A. § 522 (d)(1) (2005).

[213] See Appendix A of this book for a chart comparing the key exemptions of each the three states discussed in this comparison.

[214] For the purposes of comparison I am treating all of these hypothetical cases as if they were able to file a

the six hypothetical cases have been chosen as being somewhat representative of typical Oklahoma chapter 7 cases, while the final case for examination is a hypothetical debtor that is based on the kinds of alleged bankruptcy abuse that were discussed by Congress when it enacted BAPCPA[215].

In these hypothetical cases there are a few common themes that I think are fairly representative of the causes for bankruptcy in the real world: (1) The inability of many Americans to pay off crippling medical bills in the event of a catastrophic illness (half of these hypothetical cases are in part seeking to discharge medical bills, a percentage

---

chapter 7 petition and were eligible under the code to use the bankruptcy exemptions in question.

[215] H. R. Rep. No. 109-30(I) at 214 (2005), *also see* H. R. Rep. No. 108-40 (I) at 595-596 (2003), *and* H. R. Rep. No. 107-3 (I) at 489 (2001), *and* H. R. Rep. No. 106-123 (I) at X78-379 (1999). The high-profile bankruptcies of Burt Reynolds, Paul Bilzerian, Marvin Warner, Martin A. Siegel, Bowie Kuhn, Dr. Carlos Garcia-Rivera, and Talmadge Wayne Tinsley were discussed in these reports for their use of generous homestead exemption laws to shield significant amounts of assets from the reach of creditors.

which is consistent with the Harvard Study that showed that half of all bankruptcies are caused in part by medical expenses[216]); (2) the use of home equity loans and credit cards to pay basic living expenses during times of economic crisis, and (3) the role of divorce and other family upheaval as being factors that may lead many debtors to bankruptcy.

---

[216] David U. Himmelstein, Elizabeth Warren, Deborah Thorne, & Steffie Woolhandler, *Illness and Injury as Contributors to Bankruptcy* Health Affairs (February 2005) *AVAILABLE AT:* http://content.healthaffairs.org/cgi/content/abstract/hlthaff.w5.63v1?maxtoshow=&HITS=10&hits=10&RESULTFORMAT=&fulltext=bankruptcy&andorexactfulltext=and&searchid=1134503355382_2537&stored_search=&FIRSTINDEX=0&resourcetype=1&journalcode=healthaff *AND AVAILABLE AT:* http://www.nacba.org/maxdocs/Illness_Contributions_To_Bankruptcy.pdf, *ALSO SEE GENERALLY:* Patrcia Neighmond, *Study: Medical Bills Spur Slew of Personal Bankruptcies* (NPR Radio broadcast, February 2, 2005) *ARCHIVED ONLINE AT:* http://www.npr.org/templates/story/story.php?storyId=4475013.

Hypothetical #1 – The debtor in this case is recently divorced single mom with three children that she has sole custody of. She is filing bankruptcy because her ex-husband is not making his court-ordered child support payments and credit card payments (the divorce court ordered that she pay the mortgage on their home while he would pay the credit cards). Her assets consist of a 3 bedroom home located on a city lot valued at $110,000 (with a mortgage balance of $65,000 remaining), a car valued at $10,000 that she drives (with a loan balance of $6,500 remains), a car valued at $1,200 that her teenaged son drives, and household goods and furnishings worth about $4,000. In bankruptcy she hopes to discharge the credit debt, but keep the notes on the house and car.

If this debtor used the Oklahoma exemptions, she would be able to keep all of her assets with the possible exception of the car that her son drives (but the trustee in bankruptcy could treat this car as being of inconsequential value or would allow her the option of "buying back" the car from the estate).

If the debtor used the Alaska property exemptions she would be able to keep her home (the equity of $45,000 is below Alaska's homestead cap of $70,200, but would run into problems with her personal property. Alaska's motor vehicle exemption covers $3,900 of equity on a vehicle worth up to $26,000. The car she drives has an equity of $3,500 (which would be fully covered by the exemption), however she would still have $1,200 of excess equity on the car her son drives. The debtor would also exceed the general personal property exemption of $3,900 since she owns household goods and furnishings valued at $4,000. The excess equity on the cars and the household goods and furnishings (worth $1,300) could be treated as being of inconsequential value or the property could be sold by the estate to get access to this excess equity.

If the debtor was a New Jersey resident, she would likely not use the state exemptions since this result in her losing the equity in her home (there is no homestead exemption in New Jersey) and would leave her with only a $1,000 personal property wildcard exemption and a $1,000 household goods and furnishings to cover her personal property. However, if she used the federal exemptions $21,625 of her home's $45,000 in equity would be protected. For her primary car (which has an equity of $3,500), she would have only $50 in excess equity, but would still have the excess equity in the second vehicle to reckon with; but her furniture of $4,000 would be covered completely by the general personal property exemption. With regard to her "wildcard exemption", she is allowed only $1,150 (which could be applied to either one of her cars or the house) since she used her entire homestead exemption.

Hypothetical debtor #1 would be best off under the Oklahoma exemptions, since she would be able to keep almost all of her assets (having only $1200 remaining in non-exempt assets). The second best treatment of the comparison states is Alaska (in which she would have $1,300 remaining in non-exempt assets). Of the three states, the debtor's worst treatment would be in New Jersey, since she likely she would have to sell her home, and only be able to keep about half of the equity that she has built up, which would leave her with $23,475 in non-exempt assets.

Hypothetical #2 – The debtors in this case are a middle-aged couple who own a failed small business. They are filing bankruptcy to discharge credit card debt (they used their credit cards to pay household bills during the recent lean times with their business), medical bills (they were unable to afford health insurance during their business start-up), as well as a mortgage they owe on a piece of commercial property in small town that they purchased when the economy was still strong and the property was worth more than it is now (the current fair market value of the property is $25,000, but they owe a remaining $40,000 on the mortgage). Besides the business assets (the commercial real estate mentioned above, as well as about $2,000 of tools and equipment that were purchased with a secured debt that exceeds the value of the equipment), their principle assets are a home worth $55,000 (encumbered by a $15,000 home equity loan that was used to finance the business start-up, located on a ¼ acre lot within the town limits), two cars worth $5,000 each (both free and clear of any encumbrance), and household goods and furnishings worth about $2,000. The debtors in this case plan to give up the commercial real estate and tools used in their business, but hope to keep their house, cars and personal property in bankruptcy.

If this couple lived in Oklahoma, they would be able to keep their home (as long as they maintained the payments on the home equity loan), their cars (both of which fall below the $7,500 exemption cap) and their household goods and furnishings.

If this couple resided in Alaska they would also be able to keep their home ($40,000 of equity would fall below the cap of $70,200 for a homestead under Alaska law), and household goods and furnishings, but would run into problems with their cars (each vehicle is worth $5,000 but the Alaska exemption only covers $3,900 of equity).

If these were New Jersey debtors, they would undoubtedly use the federal exemptions, since they would lose their home and cars (but would be able to retain their household goods and furnishings by stacking the personal property wildcard and the household goods and furnishings exemptions). Under the federal exemptions, this couple would be stuck with having $18,375 in excess equity in their home, $3,100 of excess equity in their vehicles, but would have their household goods and furnishings safe. While the debtors do have some options with regards to the wildcard exemption (since the debtor's home will likely be sold, they could elect to not apply a portion of their homestead exemption towards the house and instead utilize the increased wildcard exemption to protect their cars), the total amount of excess equity will still be $20,325.

For hypothetical debtor #2, the best state's exemptions would be Oklahoma's exemptions which would protect 100% of the assets that these debtors want to keep; the second choice would be Alaska's exemption would leave the debtors with $2,200 of unprotected excess equity; and the worst choice would be New Jersey, since the application of the federal exemptions in New Jersey in this case would result in $20,325 in unprotected excess equity.

Hypothetical #3 – The debtor in this case is a single man who used to work for a local manufacturer, but has recently been laid off. He now works part-time at Wal-Mart and also does a side business as a "shade tree mechanic" in his community. He is filing bankruptcy because he know longer can make his credit card payments on his current income. He also recently had his truck repossessed (and will owe a deficiency on it) and is also two months behind on his child support obligations. His primary assets consist of 20 year old trailer home (free and clear, worth $7,000) located on a rented lot, $6,000 worth of automotive tools, a car worth $800, and $300 worth of household goods and furnishings. This debtor hopes to discharge his credit card debt as well as the deficiency on the truck repossession, so that he can support himself and be able to make his child support obligations.

If this was an Oklahoma debtor he would be in good shape after bankruptcy. His trailer home[217], car, tools and household items would all be covered under Oklahoma's generous property exemptions.

In Alaska, this debtor would be able to protect his home,[218] and car using the exemptions set for those classes of property. Then if this debtor applied the tools of the trade exemption ($3,640) to his automotive mechanic tools (valued at $6,000) and then applied his remaining general personal property exemption ($3,900 minus $300 worth of household furnishings) to the excess equity on the tools, there would be no remaining excess equity and the debtor's assets would be completely secure.

---

[217] OKLA. STAT. ANN. Tit. 31(A)(2) (2005).

[218] ALASKA STAT. ' 09.38.010(a) (2005), (2005), *Also see* ALASKA ADMIN. CODE Tit. 8, § 95.030 (2005). "(A)n individual is entitled to an exemption as a homestead of the individual's interest in property in this state used as the principle resident of the individual…" Since this statute does not specify "real property", then the trailer home is likely exempt under Alaska law.

If this debtor was in New Jersey, he would definitely use the federal exemptions, since the state exemptions leave unprotected his trailer and most of the value in his other property (New Jersey provides for a $1,000 exemption for household goods and furnishings which would be sufficient to cover his furniture, but beyond this only provides for a $1,000 wildcard exemption to cover $6,000 of tools and an $800 car). If the debtor, however, used the federal exemptions his debtor's home would be protected (using only $7,000 of the allowed $21,625 homestead exemption, which results in $10,825 being added to his wildcard exemption). His car and household furnishings would both fit under the relevant exemptions. The value of his tools (worth $6,000), however, exceeds the exemption ($2,175) for tools of the trade, however with his wildcard exemption the excess equity is protected, with the end result being that the debtor would be able to keep all of his assets in bankruptcy.

In this hypothetical, the debtor would receive equal treatment in each of the three comparison states, in that he would be able to keep all of his assets in bankruptcy.

Hypothetical #4 – The debtors in this case are a family of 5 who live on a small farm (160 acres is owned, while another 480 acres is leased). The husband works on the farm (which has lost money over the last 2 years) while the wife works as a teacher in a nearby school, where their three children attend. The family's principal assets include their land (free and clear, valued at $240,000), a small tractor with implements (with a value of $12,000), 50 head of beef cattle (valued at $20,000), 80 chickens (valued at $240), 5 guns (worth $1200 total), 1 horse (worth $2000), a pickup (worth $12,000 but $19,000 is owed on it) a car (free and clear, worth $6,000), and households goods and furnishings worth about $600. The family also owns approximately $500 worth of animal feed. The couple's debts include $65,000 in unsecured consumer debt, $45,000 on a deficiency for a tractor that was repossessed, and $35,000 in medical bills for a child who recently died from a terminal illness.

If this farm family lived in Oklahoma, their land, vehicles (assuming that the couple was able to keep up the payment on the pickup), the chickens, the horse, animal feed, the guns, and household goods and furnishings would be absolutely exempt. The problems for the family would come from the tractor and implements (there would be $2,000 of excess equity), and the cattle (worth $20,000) since unfortunately Oklahoma's exemption for cattle only covers "5 milk cows and calves" and does not provide an exemption for beef cattle.[219]

If this family resided in Alaska, they would face much harsher treatment under the law, since their land is worth $240,000 and Alaska's homestead exemption only covers $70,200 of equity. The car would also be at risk with $2,100 of excess equity (however, the family could sell this car pre-filing and then buy two cars with an equity of $3,900 each which would be both protected), as

---

[219] In re Rodney James Luckinbill, 163 B.R. 856 (W.D. Okla. 1994). Cattle breed that are bred for beef instead of milk production are no covered by Oklahoma's exemption law for milk cattle and calves.

well as the tractor with implements (worth $12,000 but the exemption only covers $3,640), the horse (using the $1,300 exemption for pets[220], they would still be left with $700 of excess equity), and the animal feed. In the end, the family would be left picking between their household goods and furnishings, livestock, and excess equity in farm equipment to be covered by only a $3,900 general personal property exemption. This family would have at least $170,000 of excess equity under the Alaska exemptions.

In New Jersey, this family would most definitely not use the state exemptions as their property (with a total equity of over $290,000) would only be protected by a total of $2000 in potential exemptions. Under the federal exemptions, the family is still left short on exemptions: the family owns $240,000 worth of land, but would only see $21,625 of it covered by the homestead exemption; the farm equipment exemption

---

[220] As of 2005, Alaska has not had interpretative case law that defines what a "pet" is for the purposes of this statute.

would only cover $2,175 of the $12,000 worth of equipment; the car (worth $6000) would have $2,550 of unprotected excess equity. With regards to the remaining property (household goods, guns and farm animals worth a total of $24,040), the family would be able to only protect $12,675 of value (using the general personal property and wildcard exemptions). This family would have at least $242,000 of excess equity under the federal exemptions used in New Jersey.

In comparing the three states, the debtors would be best served by the Oklahoma exemptions (which leave only $22,000 in unprotected excess equity); the family's second (but far inferior) choice would be Alaska (assuming the worst case scenario, the debtors would have over $170,000 in unprotected excess equity); and their last choice would be New Jersey (which would leave the debtor's with $242,000 in unprotected excess equity).

Hypothetical #5 – The debtors in this case are an elderly couple who have recently been saddled with devastating medical bills totaling over $250,000. The husband had worked as an attorney and his wife was an unpaid staff member at their church, until the wife fell ill with cancer. Over the last year (while the wife has been undergoing chemo therapy), the husband has been unable to work due to his wife's need for him to serve as her caretaker, so at this point the couple's only income are their SSI payments. The couple's assets consist of a home (valued at $95,000, but encumbered by a home equity loan for $35,000 that was taken out by the couple to pay bills over the last year when the husband was not working), a car (free and clear, worth $4,500), the husband's law books and office computer (worth $2,000) and household goods and furnishings (valued at $800).

Under the generous Oklahoma exemption law, this couple would have all of their assets protected, but if this couple were in Alaska, their treatment would also be fairly generous with a few limitations: all of the equity in their home would be protected; $3,900 of equity in the couple's car worth $4,500 would be protected, and the law books, computer, and household goods and furnishings would be completely protected.

Under New Jersey law this couple would not use the state exemptions (since they only cover a total of $2,000 of personal property) and would instead opt to use the federal exemptions which would protect $21,625 of the home's equity (leaving $38,375 of equity unprotected), $3,450 of the vehicle's equity would be protected (leaving $1,050 of equity unprotected), all of the value of the law office computer and books would be protected under the tools of trade exemption , and all of the household goods and furnishings would be saved too. The debtors could then use the wildcard exemption to cover the excess equity in their vehicle.

In comparing these three states, Oklahoma is undoubtedly the most generous option for the debtors since all of their assets would be protected. A close second would be Alaska since only $600 of excess equity would remain. In dead last place would be New Jersey, since there would be $38,375 remaining in unprotected excess equity under this state's exemptions Also worth mentioning is that this couple would have to move from their home, which would be a tremendous blow in the midst of their terrible health situation.

Hypothetical #6 – The debtor in this hypothetical case is based roughly on some of the celebrity bankruptcies that were discussed by Congress in the enactment of BAPCPA, in which a debtor with massive debt is able to shelter significant amounts of assets by use of the homestead exemption law. While the new code revisions have placed some limitations on this practice[221], the use of the homestead exemptions would still be possible in some cases, so this hypothetical is designed with such a case in mind.

The debtor in hypothetical #6 is famous movie actor who has been domiciled in his native state since his birth in the 1930's. His assets consist of a $2.5 million mansion located on a ¼ acre lot within the corporate limits of the state's largest city (purchased

---

[221] *See supra* pages 2-3.

by the debtor with cash seven years ago). The debtor's other assets include a classic corvette (worth $35,000), household furnishings (worth $120,000), a private jet worth ($1.5 million), a ranch located in another state (worth $1.3 million but encumbered by a mortgage of $700,000), memorabilia from his past films (valued at $150,000), and a restaurant (valued at $1.7 million but encumbered by secured debts worth more than the value of the business). The debtor's liabilities consist of over $10 million in debts incurred through extravagant living, and the loss of millions in the debtor's failed restaurant business. The debtor hopes to keep his house, furnishings, corvette, jet and memorabilia while walking away from the restaurant.

If this debtor was an Oklahoma domiciliary, he would be able to secure a substantial portion of his assets. His home would be completely protected. His other unencumbered assets would be at risk however since his corvette's value ($35,000) exceeds the motor vehicle exemption, his private jet would not be exempt at all (he could argue that this is a "tool of the trade" as an actor but even if he got this long-shot exemption it would only cover a miniscule portion of its value), and his highly valued household furnishings and memorabilia would likely be seen as not being "held primarily for personal, family or household use"[222] and therefore not exempt (other than the portion of the household furnishings that are held for personal use).

If this debtor was an Alaska resident, his treatment would differ significantly. His multi-million dollar home would only receive $70,200 in homestead exemption protection (the practical result being that his home would likely be sold and he would be given $70,200 to purchase a much smaller home), his corvette would not be exempt at all (the $3,900 of protected equity only protects vehicles with a total value of less than $26,000, hence he would be best off to sell the corvette pre-petition and then purchase a car that would comply with the

---

[222] *In re* Reid 757 F.2d 230 (10TH CIR. 1985). This case found that a debtor could not claim as exempt household furnishings or "pictures and portraits" a set of paintings that were valued at approximately $187,000.

Alaska "luxury car" prohibition in its exemptions), his jet would arguably not be exempt (the $3,640 tools of the trade exemption wouldn't even make a dent in the plane's value), and his household furnishings and memorabilia (with a total value of $270,000) would be protected by only $3,900 in total exemptions (using the household goods and furnishings and the general personal property exemptions).

If this debtor was a New Jersey resident, his treatment would even be more austere. Using the federal exemptions, he would only have $21,625 in a homestead exemption, $3,450 for the car, $2,175 for tools of trade (which he might be able to apply towards his jet), and $10,825 left in exemptions to cover his household goods and furnishings and memorabilia (with a total value of $270,000).

In all of the comparison states, hypothetical debtor #6 will lose significant amounts of assets, but he will still be able to protect over $2.5 million in assets as an Oklahoma debtor, while Alaska will only permit him to shield $81,640 in assets (assuming he sold his corvette and bought a cheaper car pre-bankruptcy) and New Jersey would leave him with only $38,075 in assets.

Hypothetical #7 – The circumstances of debtor #7 are identical to that of the debtor in hypothetical #6, except for one key wrinkle: debtor #7 moved to his current state of residence 3 years ago (1,095 days). At this same time he sold his previous home ("homestead") and purchased his current homestead.

Based on this fact pattern, according to 522(b)(3)(A), debtor #7 met the "730 day rule" and can take the exemptions of his current state of residence, however the debtor would fail the "1215 day test" of §522(p)(1) and hence would have his homestead exemption capped at $136, 875.

As an Oklahoma resident, Debtor #7 would keep a lot of his assets, but would lose more than 90% of his homestead's $2.5 million equity, so it would make sense that the Debtor would simply delay filing bankruptcy (being able to still enjoy the protections of the state homestead exemption outside of bankruptcy in the meantime), but of course other factors (i.e. wage garnishments) may make this impossible.

As a resident of Alaska or New Jersey, Debtor #7 would not receive any different treatment than Debto #6 would receive.

In examining all of the above hypothetical cases, it is clear that Oklahoma provided the best treatment for the debtor of any of the other comparison states (except for hypothetical #3 in which the exemptions of all three comparison states would have protected 100% of the debtor's assets). If one argues that the Congressional intent is to allow states to set their own balance between the interests of creditors and debtors, and that one argues that Oklahoma's desired balance is one that is very pro-debtor, then it would appear that Oklahoma's exemptions do function today in a manner that fulfills this legislative intention.

However, one could argue that in light of the passage of BAPCPA, that Congress has intended to eliminate the abusive use of bankruptcy by wealthy debtors seeking to discharge large amounts of debt while retaining substantial assets. If this is the Congressional intent of the new Bankruptcy code, then one could make a strong argument that Oklahoma's exemption laws function to permit an abusive debtor (who fits under the loopholes of BAPCPA) to "make off like a bandit" with substantial assets while leaving the creditors without recourse. The problem of course is that if Oklahoma tightened up its exemptions (particularly the generous homestead exemption), that the debtors punished would not only be the abusive debtors like hypothetical case #6 (see above), but also would punish retirees struggling to pay their medical bills (such as the debtors in hypothetical #5), family farmers whose assets on paper may seem large until one realizes that without those assets a family farm is not be profitable (see hypothetical case #4 above), or hard-working people whose only major asset is their home (see hypothetical cases #1 & 2 above).

Another issue worth noting is the difference between Debtors #6 and #7. One could argue that Debtor #6 does not deserve any better treatment under Oklahoma law than does Debtor #7, but one could argue that Debtor #6 has a deeper attachment to his current state of residence (and has paid more taxes to that state) and hence should be entitled to a deeper level of protection from creditors.

Chapter 3 - Conclusion and suggestions for change

The previous examination of the history of the Oklahoma exemptions shows that Oklahoma historically has a long history of providing generous homestead and personal property exemptions to debtors (and a long history of reexamining those exemptions and rewriting them to fulfill the intended general purposes of the law under new contexts that arise due to changing socio-economic conditions), and the examination of the treatment of debtors in bankruptcy under Oklahoma exemptions as compared to those of others states has shown that Oklahoma's exemptions function in the present-context in large part as designed.

Thanks to BAPCPA, Oklahoma's legislature faces a new challenge. If Oklahoma is to continue to serve as a safe haven for its residents who are harried and harassed by oppressive creditors, it is time to consider changes to both the exemption laws and to other related statutory provisions to maintain Oklahoma's historically set balance that places the interests of creditors subordinate to the future chances for success of the debtor.

One category of debtor that is most desperately in need of legislative relief are those debtors who do not own significant assets of any kind (who either rent or live with extended family). Much like the "dirt farmers" of early Oklahoma history, many of today's debtors do not have access to the capital that needed to pull themselves out of poverty (i.e. the ability to afford higher education or to be able to build equity in a home) and do not have access to credit except by means of resorting to high-interest paycheck loan companies, pawn shops and other forms of predatory lending.

While the underlying socio-economic issues at stake are regrettably beyond the scope of this book, I would propose that there are three things the state legislature could do now to alleviate the suffering of this class of debtors. First, the legislature should abolish the future use of wage garnishments as a method of debt collection. This needs to be done as wage garnishments serve to push many desperate debtors over the brink of financial ruin (and also serve to reward creditors who are unwilling to work with a struggling debtor) and frankly are not needed in today's world, since three states (Pennsylvania, South Carolina, Texas) function well without this form of garnishment.[223]

---

[223] *State Collection Laws* CARREON AND ASSOCIATES (1997, 2005) *AVAILABLE AT:*
http://www.carreonandassociates.com/articles/collect
ionlaws.htm.

Secondly, the state legislature should consider strategies by which to regulate (or even outlaw) high interest loan companies (so called "paycheck lending"). There are of course Interstate Commerce challenges to regulating this industry, but if state regulation is proven ineffective it may be time to consider applying pressure to Oklahoma's US Congressional delegation to seek federal regulation to block these companies from exploiting the most desperately poor.

Third the legislature should consider adding state law protections to debtors to be free from harassing phone calls, including an outright ban on creditors calling a debtor at his or her place of employment. While federal regulations do exist in this area, it would seem that state regulations might also be helpful (particularly given the recent success experienced from state restrictions on phone calls to Oklahomans by telemarketers).[224]

---

[224] *See* 15 OKL.ST.ANN. § 775B, *also see The*

Beyond these most extreme cases, I would also recommend that Oklahoma significantly rewrite its agricultural exemptions. Current law protects the homestead, but will leave often unprotected the machinery needed to work that land (even the most basic of farm equipment often will exceed the valuation cap of the Oklahoma exemptions) and the animals that might be raised on that land (as discussed above, Oklahoma exemptions only protect farm animals raised for subsistence purposes and not those raised for monetary profit.) Rewritten agricultural exemptions should take into account the significant capital investment required for family farmers and do a better job of actually protecting the ability of a family farmer to make a living on the farm.[225] In

---

Attorney General's Telemarketer Restriction Act Consumer Registry (2005) AVAILABLE AT: http://www.oag.state.ok.us/oagweb.nsf/DoNotCall?OpenPage.

[225] To avoid the issues of abuse by debtors attempting to abusively shield assets, these proposed increased agricultural exemptions might require that a farmer to have either owned the equipment in question for at least three years, or to pledge to use the equipment in

like manner, for small business owners whose primary source of livelihood is their business[226], I would also recommended increasing the exemption for tools of trade, as well as possibly adding an exemption for business inventory with a set dollar cap.

Oklahoma should also consider using an inflation-adjusting method of adopting the dollar caps on personal property exemptions. Two of the jurisdictions that were used in the above comparison (Alaska and Federal) use an automatic cost-of-living based method to fix the dollar figures on exemption caps, and it does make a real difference. For instance in 2005 (when I wrote the original version of this article), the Alaska exemption cap for equity in an automobile was set at $3,750. Today (in 2012) the exemption is set at $3,900, a difference of 4%. During that same period, Oklahoma's exemption for an equity has

---

question for at least three years.

[226] I would recommend that this exemption only apply to debtors who actually are making a living with their business assets, so as to avoid allowing abusive debtors to shield assets through sham businesses.

remained at $7,500. One could argue that it is better to leave these changes up to the legislature, but this poses the potential danger that the legislature will not act when it needs to act and then will be forced to make drastic changes when the need is to great too ignore. A prime example of this was when Oklahoma took the long-overdue step of increasing its automobile exemption from $3,000 to $7,500 in 2005 (an increase of 150%).[227]

With regards to all debtors generally, other measures that I would recommend would include: (1) adding a statutory limitation on the percentage of a homestead that can be mortgaged through a home equity loan, and (2) consider adding personal property exemptions to the Oklahoma Constitution, either by providing an exemption valuation floor in the Constitution for personal property or by utilizing an inflation-adjusting method. This change to the Oklahoma Constitution would be a radical step, but it would serve an important purpose by protecting the financial

---

[227] OKLA. STAT. ANN. Tit. 31(A)(13) (2005).

resources of Oklahomans from future state legislatures that may want to roll back these historically important personal property exemption provisions.

APPENDIX A: Key Bankruptcy Exemptions

Oklahoma

- Homestead Exemption: 1 acre (urban)/160 acres (rural) of any value[228]
- Motor Vehicle: $7500[229]
- Tools of the Trade: $10,000[230]
- Wages and Earnings: 75% of current wages[231]
- Personal Property: Household goods and furnishings of unlimited value, [232] $4,000 clothing,[233] $3,000 in wedding and anniversary rings[234], $2000 in guns
- Farm Equipment: $10,000[235]

---

[228] *See* Okla. Const. Art. XII, *also see* OKLA. STAT. ANN. Tit. 31(A)(2) (2005).

[229] OKLA. STAT. ANN. Tit. 31(A)(13) (2005).

[230] OKLA. STAT. ANN. Tit. 31(A)(5) (2005).

[231] OKLA. STAT. ANN. Tit. 31(A)(18) (2005).

[232] OKLA. STAT. ANN. Tit. 31(A)(3) (2005).

[233] OKLA. STAT. ANN. Tit. 31(A)(7) (2005).

[234] OKLA. STAT. ANN. Tit. 31(A)(8) (2005).

[235] OKLA. STAT. ANN. Tit. 31(A)(5) (2005).

- Farm Animals and Supplies: 5 milk cows and calves, 100 chickens, 2 horses, 2 saddles and 2 bridles, 10 hogs, 20 sheep, provisions and forage for one year[236]
- Wildcard: None

Alaska

- Homestead Exemption: $70,200[237]
- Motor Vehicle: $3,900 of equity on a vehicle worth up to $26,000 total value[238]
- Tools of the Trade: $3,640 (covered under a single exemption for "tools of the trade and implements")[239]
- Wages and Earnings: Weekly net earnings up to $456, or up to $716 if sole wage earner in a household: If no regular pay, up to $1,820 paid in any month, or $2,860 if sole wage earner in household. [240]

---

[236] OKLA. STAT. ANN. Tit. 31(A)(10-12) (2005).

[237] ALASKA STAT. § 09.38.010 (2005), *Also see* ALASKA ADMIN. CODE Tit. 8, § 95.030 (2008).

[238] ALASKA STAT. § 09.38.020 (2005), *Also see* ALASKA ADMIN. CODE Tit. 8, § 95.030 (2008).

[239] ALASKA STAT. § 09.38.020 (2005), *Also see* ALASKA ADMIN. CODE Tit. 8, § 95.030 (2008).

- Personal Property: $3,900 general personal property, $1,300 jewelry, $1,300 pets[241]
- Farm Equipment: $3,640 (covered under a single exemption for "tools of the trade and implements")[242]
- Farm Animals and Supplies: None [243]
- Wildcard: None

New Jersey (state law exemptions)
- Homestead Exemption: None
- Motor Vehicle: None[244]
- Tools of the Trade: None[245]

---

[240] ALASKA STAT. § 09.38.030 (2005), *Also see* ALASKA ADMIN. CODE Tit. 8, § 95.030 (2008).

[241] ALASKA STAT. § 09.38.020 (2005).

[242] ALASKA STAT. § 09.38.020 (2005), *Also see* ALASKA ADMIN. CODE Tit. 8, § 95.030 (2008).

[243] There is no farm animal exemption under the Alaska exemptions; however there is a $1000 exemption for pets. There has been no case law as of 2005 that has defined what the word "pet" means under this provision.

[244] While there is no separate exemption for this category, items in this category could be included as part of the $1000 general personal property exemption.

[245] While there is no separate exemption for this category, items in this category could be included as part of the $1000 general personal property

- Wages and Earnings: None[246]
- Personal Property: $1000 household goods and furnishings,[247] $1000 general personal property, [248]clothing of unlimited value[249]
- Farm Equipment: None[250]
- Farm Animals and Supplies: None[251]
- Wildcard: None

Federal Exemptions (allowed for use in New Jersey in lieu of state exemptions)
- Homestead Exemption: $21,625 in "in real property or personal

---

exemption.

[246] While there is no separate exemption for this category, items in this category could be included as part of the $1000 general personal property exemption.

[247] N.J. STAT. ANN. § 2A:26-4 (2005).

[248] N.J. STAT. ANN. § 2A:17-19 (2005).

[249] N.J. STAT. ANN. § 2A:17-19 (2005).

[250] While there is no separate exemption for this category, items in this category could be included as part of the $1000 general personal property exemption.

[251] While there is no separate exemption for this category, items in this category could be included as part of the $1000 general personal property exemption.

property that the debtor or a dependent of the debtor uses as a residence[252]

- Motor Vehicle: $3,450[253]
- Tools of the Trade: $2,175 (covered under a single exemption for "Implements, books and tools of trade ")[254]
- Wages and Earnings: None
- Personal Property: $1,450 in jewelry, $11,525 general personal property (but not to exceed $550 in any one item),[255]
- Farm Equipment: $2,175 (covered under a single exemption for "Implements, books and tools of trade "[256]
- Farm Animals and Supplies: Included under general personal property exemption[257]

---

[252] 11 U.S.C.A. § 522 (d)(1) (2005).

[253] 11 U.S.C.A. § 522 (d)(2) (2005).

[254] 11 U.S.C.A. § 522 (d)(6) (2005).

[255] 11 U.S.C.A. § 522 (d)(3) (2005).

[256] 11 U.S.C.A. § 522 (d)(6) (2005).

[257] 11 U.S.C.A. § 522 (d)(3) (2005).

- Wildcard: $1,150 and up to $10,825 of the value of the unused homestead exemption[258]

APPENDIX B: Value of historic dollar figures in 2010 dollars[259]

$50 (1906) = $1,250
$100 (1906) = $2,500
$200 (1906) = $5,000
$500 (1906) = $12,500
$1000 (1906) = $25,000
$1500 (1906) = $37,500

[258] 11 U.S.C.A. § 522 (d)(5) (2005).

[259]These numbers were based on the valuation calculated using the purchasing power calculator at: http://www.measuringworth.com/uscompare/relative value.php.

APPENDIX C: Maps

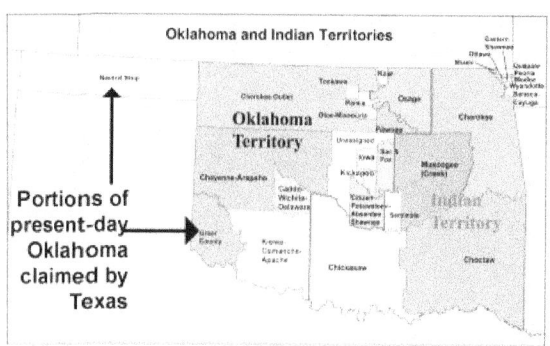

Map 1

---

260 Map 1 is a modified version of the map found at:
https://en.wikipedia.org/wiki/File:Okterritory.png,
used and modified with permission.

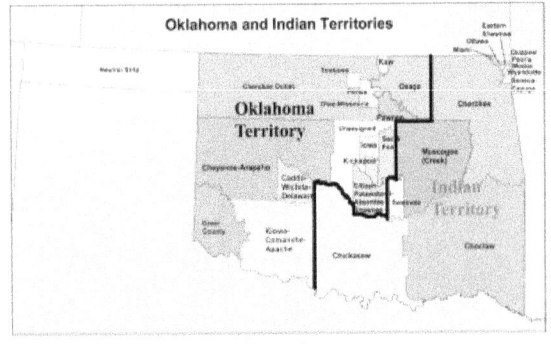

Map 2

261

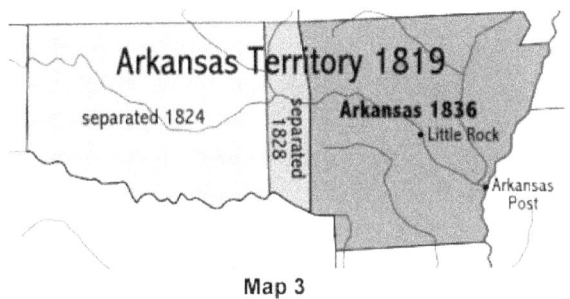

Map 3

262

[262] Map 3 is a modified version of the map found at:
https://en.wikipedia.org/wiki/File:Arkansasterritory.P
NG, used and modified with permission.

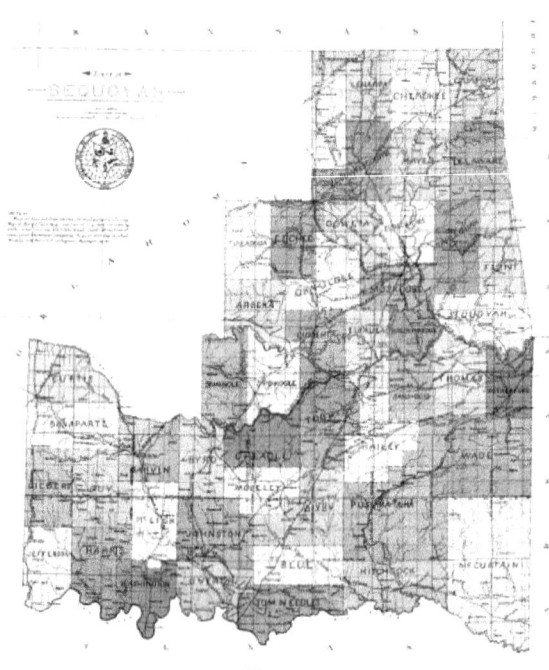

Map 4

---

263 Map 4 is a modified version of the map found at: https://en.wikipedia.org/wiki/File:Sequoyah_map.jpg , used and modified with permission.

About the author:

James M. Branum is a solo attorney in Oklahoma. He also serves as the Minister of Peace & Justice of Joy Mennonite Church in Oklahoma City and as the advising attorney of the Oklahoma Center for Conscience and Peace Research.

He is a past chair of the Military Law Task Force of the National Lawyers Guild. He has taught continuing legal education seminars on a variety of topics in several states. He was the named one of the 2010 "Legal Rebels" by the American Bar Journal.

He is the author of the book *US Army AWOL Defense: A Practice Guide and Formbook*.

His website can be found at www.jmbranum.com.

Other Books available from Green Corn Press:

US Army AWOL Defense: A Practice Guide and Form Book

by James M. Branum

Order today from all major booksellers or at our website www.greencornpress.com

www.ingramcontent.com/pod-product-compliance
Lightning Source LLC
Chambersburg PA
CBHW061511180526
45171CB00001B/136